ASIAN DEVELOPMENT BANK
TRUST FUNDS
REPORT 2020
INCLUDES GLOBAL AND SPECIAL FUNDS

AUGUST 2021

ADB

ASIAN DEVELOPMENT BANK

CONTENTS

TABLES AND FIGURES

ABBREVIATIONS

ADB	Asian Development Bank
ASEAN	Association of Southeast Asian Nations
COVID-19	coronavirus disease
CWRD	Central and West Asia Department
DMC	developing member country
OP	operational priority
PSOD	Private Sector Operations Department
TA	technical assistance

FOREWORD

The coronavirus disease (COVID-19) continues to pose an unprecedented challenge to the development aid community. The pandemic has claimed millions of lives, devastated economies, and, in many cases, reversed years of development gains. Clearly, it calls for stronger global cooperation. The health, economic, and social crises created by the pandemic have increased demand for additional foreign aid, especially for emergency aid delivered quickly and efficiently. Official development assistance has been central in both limiting the spread of the virus and mitigating its economic impact. In 2020, ADB committed a record $31.6 billion in operations with an additional $16.4 billion in cofinancing to provide much needed financing for the immediate pandemic response and recovery, while continuing to help economies meet their long-term development agendas.

Pooled funding—such as trust funds, global funds, and special funds—remains a vital tool in providing needed aid. It plays an essential role in coordinating and harmonizing development interventions, even during a pandemic. Pooled funding offers three critical services as it (i) mobilizes financial resources across various sources, (ii) reduces fragmentation or duplication of aid initiatives by supporting coordinated assistance delivery, and (iii) leverages donors' knowledge and resources to meet development challenges. For ADB, it remains a valuable way to efficiently and effectively mobilize and deploy external resources into our operations.

By the end of 2020, cumulative donor contributions to ADB reached $8.8 billion. These significant contributions help sustain support for issues such as disaster risk management, clean energy, private sector development, gender and development, good governance, information technology, poverty reduction, and regional trade. Under our long-term Strategy 2030, ADB will further strengthen our partnerships for funding, collaboration, and knowledge-sharing. We will strategically work with our partners to promote innovation, deliver high quality grant and loan projects, and to develop the capacity of our developing members.

Trust funds are instrumental in advancing our knowledge agenda as they support technical assistance. In 2020, $143 million or about 30% of ADB technical assistance were financed by trust funds, global funds, and special funds. They helped promote pilot projects, scale up successful pilot projects, replicate projects across borders, apply innovative technology solutions, build capacity, and offer policy advice and research. Trust funds contribute to our objective of becoming an innovative and valued knowledge bank—one that disseminates specialized, evidence-based knowledge to help achieve a prosperous, inclusive, resilient, and sustainable Asia and Pacific region.

Trust funds quickly became an integral part of ADB's COVID-19 emergency support. In 2020, our donors committed $170.6 million, of which $79 million was deployed for pandemic response projects and technical assistance by end-December. This included $55 million for rapid-deployment grants for immediate humanitarian and health emergency expenses to 29 developing members and through regional activities.

Supporting hard-hit economies, replacing jobs lost, protecting the vulnerable and strengthening overwhelmed health systems will be even more of an operational and financial challenge. Thus, trust fund management will remain a key part of ADB operations.

The *Trust Funds Report 2020* will help you become more familiar with what ADB is doing. It represents the continuing trust and enduring partnerships we have with our donors. As we prepare to live under a new (and next) normal, ADB will continue to collaborate and cooperate with donors to offer effective solutions and products that deliver benefits and generate results to improve the lives of the people in Asia and the Pacific.

Bambang Susantono
Vice-President
Knowledge Management and Sustainable Development
Asian Development Bank

I. INTRODUCTION

ABOUT THE REPORT

This report provides information on the status of trust funds (both stand-alone and those under financing partnership facilities), global funds, and special funds on a yearly basis. It highlights indicators including contributions committed, project commitments, disbursements, and net available balance for active funds. The report also assesses how the various funds have supported ADB's response and recovery efforts to the coronavirus disease (COVID-19) pandemic, as well as the seven operational priorities (OP) of ADB's Strategy 2030.

DEFINITION OF KEY TERMS

A trust fund is a means of channeling cofinancing resources to finance various projects and activities that meet certain eligibility criteria. It may be financed by a single partner or supported by multiple partners or donors. A trust fund may also be created as a stand-alone fund or established under a financing partnership facility (FPF).

Financing partnership facilities are ADB's operational mechanisms for strategic, long-term, and multi-partner cooperation. FPFs link various forms of assistance in a coordinated manner for well-defined purposes.

A global fund is a fund for which an organization acts as its global trustee or administrator. It typically leverages a variety of public and private resources in support of international initiatives, enabling the development partner community to provide a direct and coordinated response to global priorities.

ADB acts as an implementing agency and signs a participation agreement for each global fund. Funds are transferred to ADB for project and program implementation and are used in accordance with ADB's policies and guidelines.

Special funds are funds defined in Article 19 of Agreement Establishing the Asian Development Bank. This report excludes the Asian Development Fund, the Technical Assistance Special Fund, and the ADB Institute Special Fund.

Data Sources

- Status of Grant and Statement of Expenditures, 31 December 2020 (Controller's Department)
- Monthly Financial Report, 31 December 2020 (Controller's Department)
- Grant Financial Information System, Technical Assistance Information System
- Cofinance Management System (Cofinance Management System, Partner Funds Division, Sustainable Development and Climate Change Department [SDCC])
- Cofinancing Database (Partner Funds Division, SDCC)
- SDCC Management Information System, 31 December 2020
- Statement of ADB Operations in 2020 (Procurement, Portfolio and Financial Management Department)
- Fund Profile Data Sheet
- eOperations classification of projects support to operational priorities (Classification started from April 2019 ADB-approved projects except (i) supplementary approvals for additional financing, and (ii) Private Sector Operations Department loans and equities. Strategy, Policy and Partnerships Department is reviewing the project's classification and may be subject to future adjustments).

II. 2020 HIGHLIGHTS

Active ADB Funds

56 Funds

5 Special Funds

6 Global Funds

45 Trust Funds

Newly Established Funds

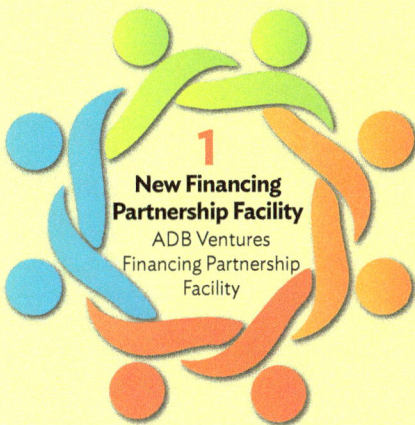

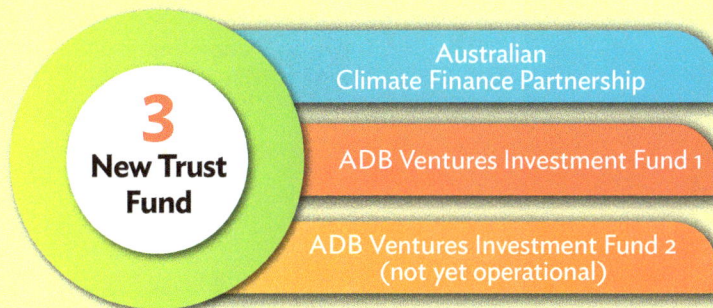

1 New Financing Partnership Facility

ADB Ventures Financing Partnership Facility

3 New Trust Fund

Australian Climate Finance Partnership

ADB Ventures Investment Fund 1

ADB Ventures Investment Fund 2 (not yet operational)

2020 Donor Contributions

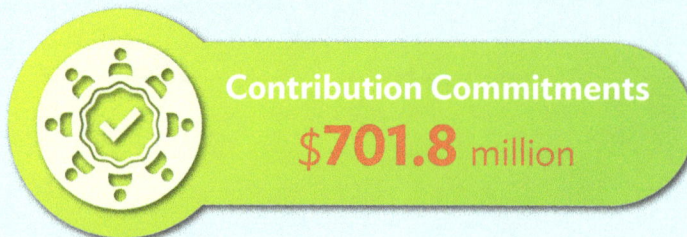

Contribution Commitments
$701.8 million

New Contributions and Fund Allocations for COVID-19 Proposals

$75 million — Japan Fund for Poverty Reduction COVID-19 Window

$75 million — Asia Pacific Disaster Response Fund support to COVID-19 response

$10 million — People's Republic of China Fund

$6.3 million — Regional Malaria and Other Communicable Disease Threats Trust Fund under the Health Financing Partnership Facility

$2.3 million — Ireland Trust Fund for Building Climate Change and Disaster Resilience in Small Island Developing States

$2 million — Republic of Korea e-Asia and Knowledge Partnership Fund

2020 Project and TA Commitments

$772 million

Total Project and TA Commitments and Direct Charges from Trust Funds, Global Funds, and Special Funds

$624 million

for **76** Investment Projects

$144 million

for **126** Technical Assistance

$4 million

for **21** Direct Charges

TA = technical assistance.

Other 2020 Accomplishments

$362.7 million

Disbursements (Projects and Direct Charges Expenditures)

122 Scholarships Awarded

2020 ACTIVE TRUST FUNDS, GLOBAL FUNDS, AND SPECIAL FUNDS PORTFOLIO

As of the end of December 2020, ADB is administering 45 trust funds and 5 special funds, of which 15 trust funds and 1 special fund are under six financing partnership facilities (Clean Energy, Health, Regional Cooperation and Integration, Urban, Water, and ADB Ventures). In addition, ADB is also participating in 6 global funds.

Of the 45 trust funds, 1 trust fund is not yet operational; 28 trust funds have balances for new projects and activities; 3 trust funds have balances for specific usage such as Afghanistan projects, certified emission reduction, and scholarship programs; 4 trust funds are for Private Sector Operations Department (PSOD) projects; 1 trust fund is active with no balance for new projects, while 8 trust funds are inactive. Inactive trust funds are either awaiting (i) completion of projects; or (ii) partner's instruction on unutilized balances. (For data analysis, the Credit Guarantee Investment Facility has been excluded due to its distinct nature. This facility provides guarantees for local currency-denominated bonds issued by investment grade companies in Association of Southeast Asian Nations [ASEAN]+3 countries.)

2020 DONOR CONTRIBUTIONS

A total of $701.8 million in contributions committed in 2020 came from 16 partners, bringing the total cumulative contribution commitments to $8.8 billion.

NEW CONTRIBUTIONS AND ALLOCATIONS FOR COVID-19 PROPOSALS

In support of ADB's effort to its developing member countries (DMCs) in combating the effects of the coronavirus disease (COVID-19) pandemic, the Government of Japan provided emergency support of $150 million through the Japan Fund for Poverty Reduction and the Asia Pacific Disaster Response Fund. In addition, $2.3 million from the Ireland Trust Fund for Building Climate Change and Disaster Resilience in Small Island Developing States was used to support the health emergency responses of small island developing states, £4.8 million was contributed by the Government of the United Kingdom to the Regional Malaria and Other Communicable Disease Threats Trust Fund to support a regional technical assistance (TA), $10 million was earmarked by the Government of the People's Republic of China (PRC) through the PRC Fund to support ADB DMCs address their COVID-19 challenges, and $2 million was set aside by the Republic of Korea e-Asia and Knowledge Partnership Fund to support a regional TA which enhanced capacities of DMCs to detect, prevent, and respond to COVID-19 and other communicable diseases.

2020 PROJECT AND TA COMMITMENTS FROM TRUST FUNDS, GLOBAL FUNDS, AND SPECIAL FUNDS

Total project and TA commitments reached $772.1 million, of which $768 million is for 201 investment projects and TA under administration, and $4.1 million are for 32 direct charges.

Active projects portfolio comprises 751 projects.[1] Breakdown of active projects are: 500 technical assistance projects, 179 investment grants, and 72 loans and equities. A total of 84 projects were financially closed in 2020, comprising 59 TAs, 22 investment grants, and 3 loans.

Disbursements for project and direct charges expenditures amounted to approximately $402.3 million in 2020, while administrative expenses amounted to $41.6 million. Administrative expenses include ADB service fees, external audit fees, staff consultants, business travel, financial expenses, and provision for credit losses, among others.

$79.3 million or 10.3% of the total project and TA commitments was for COVID-19 response and recovery support. A total of $61.7 million of COVID-19 support went to investment projects while the remaining $17.6 million supported technical assistance.

A.   NUMBER OF TRUST FUNDS

The total number of ADB-administered funds in 2020 is 56, which includes 45 trust funds, 6 global funds and 5 other special funds. During the year, the ADB Ventures Financing Partnership Facility was established, bringing the total number of ADB-administered financing partnership facilities to six. Three new trust funds were also established: the ADB Ventures Investment Fund 1, the ADB Ventures Investment Fund 2[2], and the Australian Climate Finance Partnership. Two trust funds were also closed during the year— the Technical Assistance Grant Fund (France) and the Cooperation Fund in Support for Managing Development Results.

B.   CONTRIBUTION COMMITMENT FROM EXTERNAL PARTNERS

ADB's partners provided commitments amounting to $701.8 million for the year. See Appendix 1 for details of 2020 contribution commitments.

C.   DISTRIBUTION OF ASSISTANCE

Total project and TA commitments reached $772.1 million, of which $768 million is for 201 investment projects and TA under administration, and $4.1 million are for 32 direct charges. This brings the cumulative project and TA commitments financed by trust funds, global funds, and other special funds to $6.6 billion. Cancellations and repayments in 2020 were approximately $180 million.

The following section shows the distribution of 2020 project and TA commitments by sector, departments, DMCs, and type of assistance.

---

[1]   Count by fund source; a project with multiple fund source is counted more than once.
[2]   Not yet operational.

Table 1: 2020 Contribution Commitment from External Partners
($ million)

Partner	Amount
Trust Funds	**466.1**
Japan	230.4
Australia	106.0
ANA Trust Fund	25.0
Canada	24.1
Republic of Korea	23.4
Finland	21.8
Clean Technology Fund	17.0
Nordic Development Fund	9.8
United Kingdom	7.2
France	1.1
Norway	0.2
Global Funds	**158.6**
Green Climate Fund	78.6
Climate Investment Funds	72.6
Global Agriculture and Food Security Program	4.0
Global Environment Facility	3.0
Global Partnership for Education	0.4
Special Funds	**77.0**
Japan	75.0
Luxembourg	2.0
Total	**701.8**

Notes:
1. Excludes 2020 ADB's allocation from ordinary capital resources net income to special funds.
2. Contribution received from Japan for the Leading Asia's Private Sector Infrastructure Fund ($100.3 million) and the Canadian Climate Fund for the Private Sector in Asia II ($22.6 million) is part of partner's commitment (Leading Asia's Private Sector Infrastructure Fund: $1.5 billion, Canadian Climate Fund for the Private Sector in Asia II: $149.4 million); Controller's Department formally recognized and recorded in ADB's system and financial statements once they are remitted by the financing partner to ADB.
3. Climate Investment Funds: Amount includes adjustment of $3 million support to Technical Assistance 9948 which was reverted from Fund 7J to 5H (reference Private Sector Operations Department memo January 2021) and additional letter of commitment from the trustee.
Source: Cofinance Management System.

By Developing Member Country

Regional projects (covering multiple countries) are the biggest recipient of trust fund, global fund, and special funds financing, with $193.12 million for 75 projects.

Figure 1: Distribution of Assistance by Developing Member Country—Trust Funds, Global Funds, and Special Funds

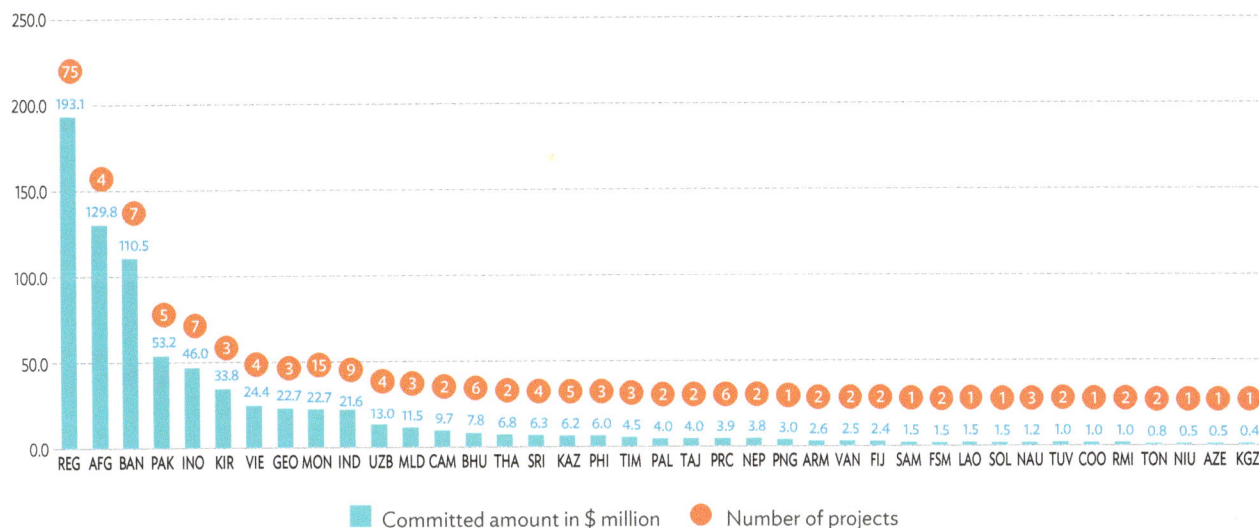

AFG = Afghanistan, ARM = Armenia, AZE = Azerbaijan, BAN = Bangladesh, BHU = Bhutan, CAM = Cambodia, COO = Cook Islands, FIJ = Fiji Islands, FSM = Federated States of Micronesia, GEO = Georgia, IND = India, INO = Indonesia, KAZ = Kazakhstan, KGZ = Kyrgyz Republic, KIR = Kiribati, LAO = Lao People's Democratic Republic, MLD = Maldives, MON = Mongolia, NAU = Nauru, NEP = Nepal, NIU = Niue, PAK = Pakistan, PAL = Palau, PHI = Philippines, PNG = Papua New Guinea, PRC = People's Republic of China, REG = regional, RMI = Marshall Islands, SAM = Samoa, SOL = Solomon Islands, SRI = Sri Lanka, TAJ = Tajikistan, THA = Thailand, TIM = Timor-Leste, TON = Tonga, TUV = Tuvalu, UZB = Uzbekistan, VAN = Vanuatu, VIE = Viet Nam.
Sources: Cofinancing Database and Statement of the Asian Development Bank's Operations in 2020.

Trust Funds

Projects across different countries or regions (regional) received the most assistance in 2020 from trust funds with $173.3 million for 60 projects. In terms of volume, Afghanistan ($129.8 million) and Bangladesh ($106.9 million) received the second and third highest financing in 2020. Mongolia (13 projects) and India (8 projects) received the second and third highest number of cofinanced projects during the year. The project "Energy Supply Improvement Investment Program—Tranche 7" in Afghanistan received the largest support in 2020 at $118 million from the Afghanistan Infrastructure Trust Fund.

Figure 2: Distribution of Assistance by Developing Member Country—Trust Funds

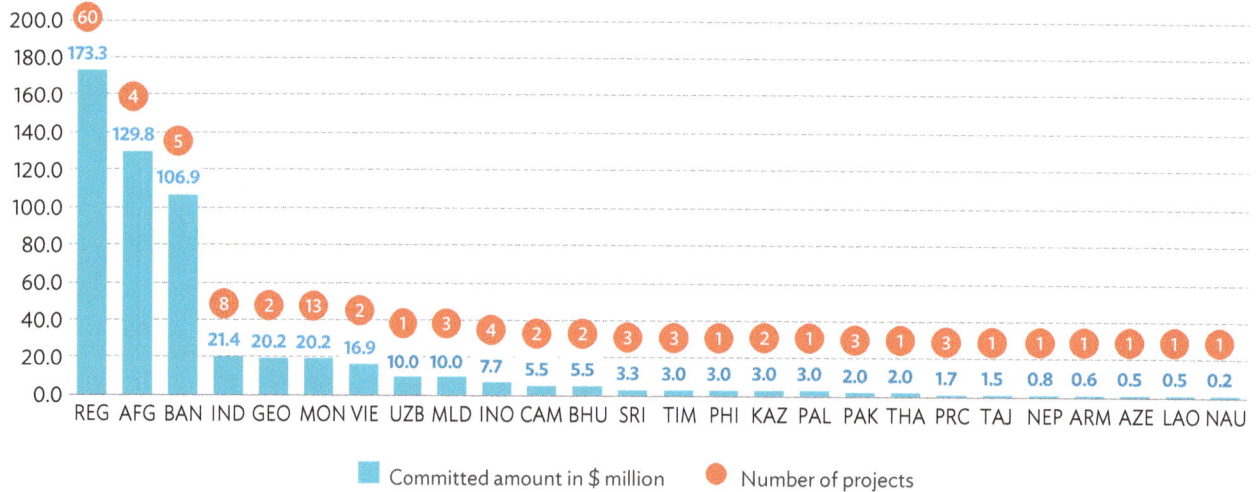

Bar chart showing committed amount in $ million (blue bars) and number of projects (orange circles) by country:

Country	Committed amount ($ million)	Number of projects
REG	173.3	60
AFG	129.8	4
BAN	106.9	5
IND	21.4	8
GEO	20.2	2
MON	20.2	13
VIE	16.9	2
UZB	10.0	1
MLD	10.0	3
INO	7.7	4
CAM	5.5	2
BHU	5.5	2
SRI	3.3	3
TIM	3.0	3
PHI	3.0	1
KAZ	3.0	2
PAL	3.0	1
PAK	2.0	3
THA	2.0	1
PRC	1.7	3
TAJ	1.5	1
NEP	0.8	1
ARM	0.6	1
AZE	0.5	1
LAO	0.5	1
NAU	0.2	1

■ Committed amount in $ million ● Number of projects

AFG = Afghanistan, ARM = Armenia, AZE = Azerbaijan, BAN = Bangladesh, BHU = Bhutan, CAM = Cambodia, GEO = Georgia, IND = India, INO = Indonesia, KAZ = Kazakhstan, LAO = Lao People's Democratic Republic, MLD = Maldives, MON = Mongolia, NAU = Nauru, NEP = Nepal, PAK = Pakistan, PAL = Palau, PHI = Philippines, PRC = People's Republic of China, REG = regional, SRI = Sri Lanka, TAJ = Tajikistan, THA = Thailand, TIM = Timor-Leste, UZB = Uzbekistan, VIE = Viet Nam.
Source: Cofinancing Database.

Global Funds

Pakistan ($49 million), Indonesia ($35 million), and Kiribati ($32 million) received the biggest support in terms of volume from global fund sources. In terms of number, regional projects (7), Indonesia and Kiribati (2 projects each) received the most global funds support. Pakistan received the biggest global funds cofinancing from the Green Climate Fund with $37.20 million loan and $11.80 million grant cofinancing for the Karachi Bus Rapid Transit Red Line Project.

Figure 3: Distribution of Assistance by Developing Member Country—Global Funds

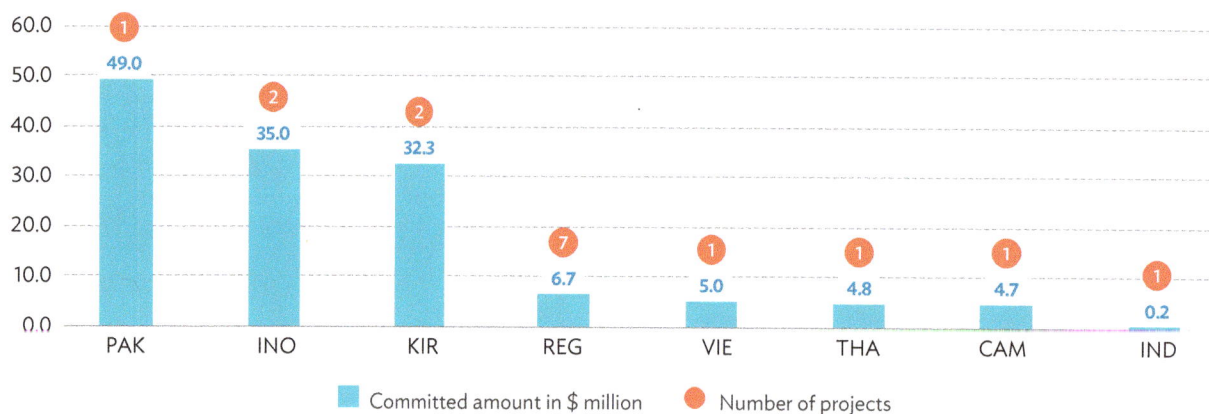

Country	Committed amount ($ million)	Number of projects
PAK	49.0	1
INO	35.0	2
KIR	32.3	2
REG	6.7	7
VIE	5.0	1
THA	4.8	1
CAM	4.7	1
IND	0.2	1

■ Committed amount in $ million ● Number of projects

CAM = Cambodia, IND = India, INO = Indonesia, KIR = Kiribati, PAK = Pakistan, REG = regional, THA = Thailand, VIE = Viet Nam.
Source: Cofinancing Database.

Special Funds

A majority of special funds went on to finance regional projects, with $13.15 million financing for 17 projects in 2020. In terms of volume, Bangladesh ($3.65 million) and Indonesia ($3.30 million) complete the top three recipients of special funds financing, while Bhutan (4 projects) and the People's Republic of China (3 projects) also received the most financing in terms of number from special funds.

Figure 4: Distribution of Assistance by Developing Member Country—Special Funds

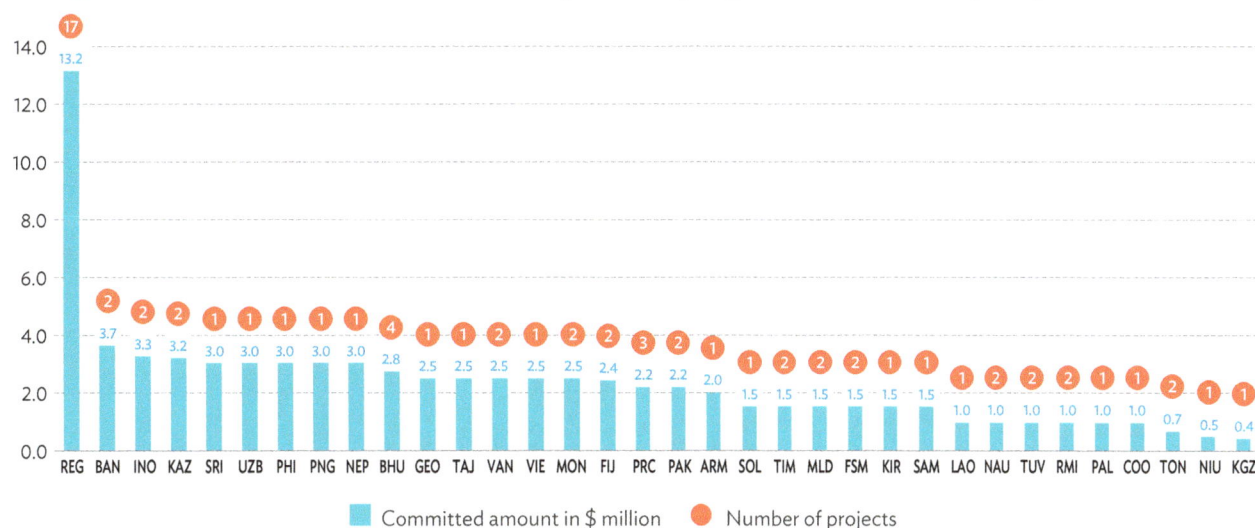

ARM = Armenia, BAN = Bangladesh, BHU = Bhutan, COO = Cook Islands, FIJ = Fiji Islands, FSM = Federated States of Micronesia, GEO = Georgia, INO = Indonesia, KAZ = Kazakhstan, KGZ = Kyrgyz Republic, KIR = Kiribati, LAO = Lao People's Democratic Republic, MLD = Maldives, MON = Mongolia, NAU = Nauru, NEP = Nepal, NIU = Niue, PAK = Pakistan, PAL = Palau, PHI = Philippines, PNG = Papua New Guinea, PRC = People's Republic of China, REG = regional, RMI = Marshall Islands, SAM = Samoa, SOL = Solomon Islands, SRI = Sri Lanka, TAJ = Tajikistan, TIM = Timor-Leste, TON = Tonga, TUV = Tuvalu, UZB = Uzbekistan, VAN = Vanuatu, VIE = Viet Nam.
Source: Statement of the Asian Development Bank's Operations in 2020.

By Department

Projects from the Central and West Asia Department (CWRD), Pacific Department, Southeast Asia Department, South Asia Department, and Sustainable Development and Climate Change Department received the most number of financing from trust fund, global fund, and special fund sources, while PSOD received the biggest financing at $272.41 million.

Figure 5: Distribution of Assistance by Department—Trust Funds, Global Funds, and Special Funds

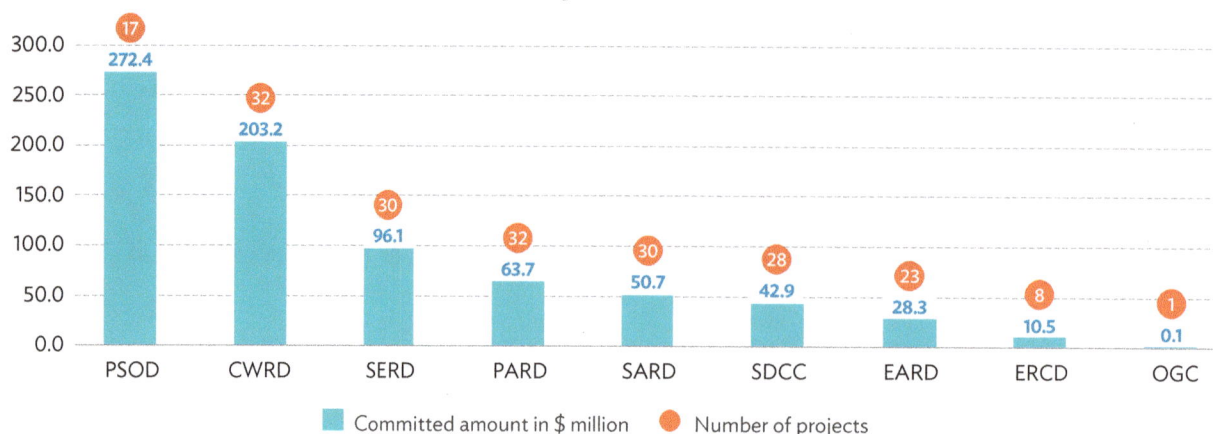

Committed amount in $ million (bars), Number of projects (circles):

Department	Committed amount ($ million)	Number of projects
PSOD	272.4	17
CWRD	203.2	32
SERD	96.1	30
PARD	63.7	32
SARD	50.7	30
SDCC	42.9	28
EARD	28.3	23
ERCD	10.5	8
OGC	0.1	1

CWRD = Central and West Asia Department, EARD = East Asia Department, ERCD = Economic Research and Regional Cooperation Department, OGC = Office of the General Counsel, PARD = Pacific Department, PSOD = Private Sector Operations Department, SARD = South Asia Department, SDCC = Sustainable Development and Climate Change Department, SERD = Southeast Asia Department.
Sources: Cofinancing Database and Statement of the Asian Development Bank's Operations in 2020.

Trust Funds

In terms of number of projects, the Sustainable Development and Climate Change Department, Southeast Asia Department, CWRD, and South Asia Department received the most cofinancing from trust funds. Their combined total represents 65% of total number of project and TA commitments in 2020.

PSOD, CWRD, and the Southeast Asia Department are the top three recipients in terms of amount from trust funds. PSOD received 48% of total commitments for 12 projects.

Figure 6: Distribution of Assistance by Department—Trust Funds

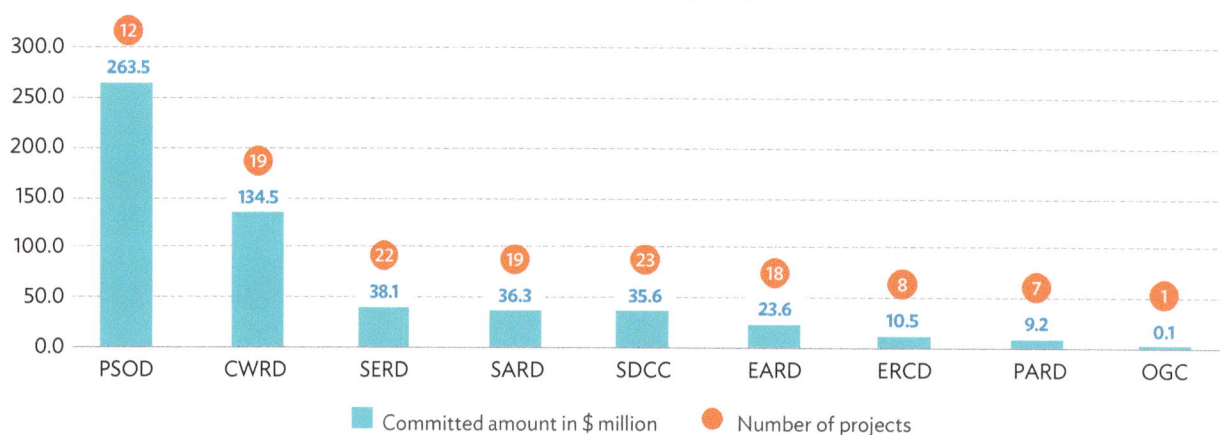

Committed amount in $ million (bars), Number of projects (circles):

Department	Committed amount ($ million)	Number of projects
PSOD	263.5	12
CWRD	134.5	19
SERD	38.1	22
SARD	36.3	19
SDCC	35.6	23
EARD	23.6	18
ERCD	10.5	8
PARD	9.2	7
OGC	0.1	1

CWRD = Central and West Asia Department, EARD = East Asia Department, ERCD = Economic Research and Regional Cooperation Department, OGC = Office of the General Counsel, PARD = Pacific Department, PSOD = Private Sector Operations Department, SARD = South Asia Department, SDCC = Sustainable Development and Climate Change Department, SERD = Southeast Asia Department.
Source: Cofinancing Database.

Global Funds

CWRD received $49.0 million or 36% of the total support for a loan and grant cofinancing for Pakistan: Karachi Bus Rapid Transit Red Line Project from the Green Climate Fund.

Figure 7: Distribution of Assistance by Department—Global Funds

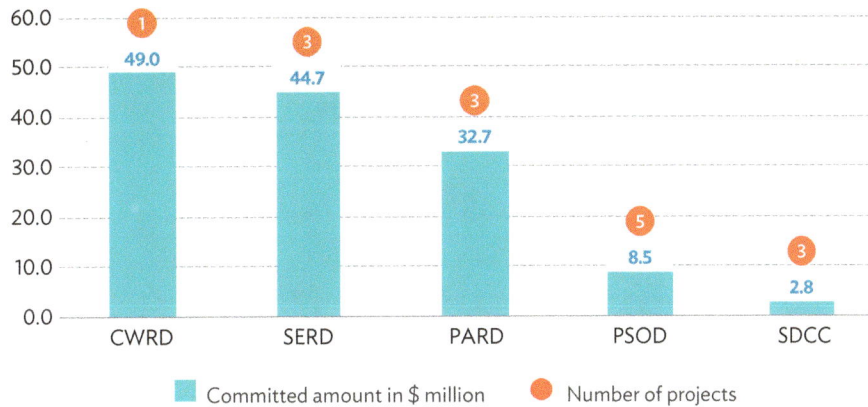

CWRD = Central and West Asia Department, PARD = Pacific Department, PSOD = Private Sector Operations Department, SDCC = Sustainable Development and Climate Change Department, SERD = Southeast Asia Department.
Source: Cofinancing Database.

Special Funds

The Pacific Department ($21.8 million for 23 projects), CWRD ($19.7 million for 14 projects), and the South Asia Department ($14.4 million for 11 projects) are the biggest department recipients of special funds financing in 2020.

Figure 8: Distribution of Assistance by Department—Special Funds

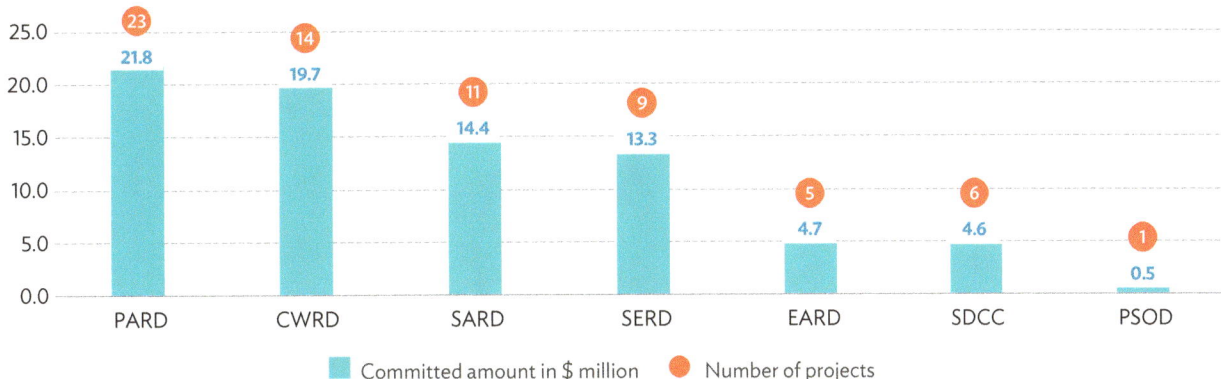

CWRD = Central and West Asia Department, EARD = East Asia Department, PARD = Pacific Department, PSOD = Private Sector Operations Department, SARD = South Asia Department, SDCC = Sustainable Development and Climate Change Department, SERD = Southeast Asia Department.
Source: Statement of the Asian Development Bank's Operations in 2020.

By Sector

In terms of volume, the Energy sector ($355.6 million), Water and Other Urban Infrastructure and Services ($128.7 million), and Health ($69.6 million) received the most assistance. Meanwhile, the Health sector recorded the most number of projects financed by trust funds, global funds, and special funds at 44 projects, followed by Energy (37 projects) and Agriculture, Natural Resources, and Rural Development (27 projects).

Figure 9: Distribution of Assistance by Sector—Trust Funds, Global Funds, and Special Funds

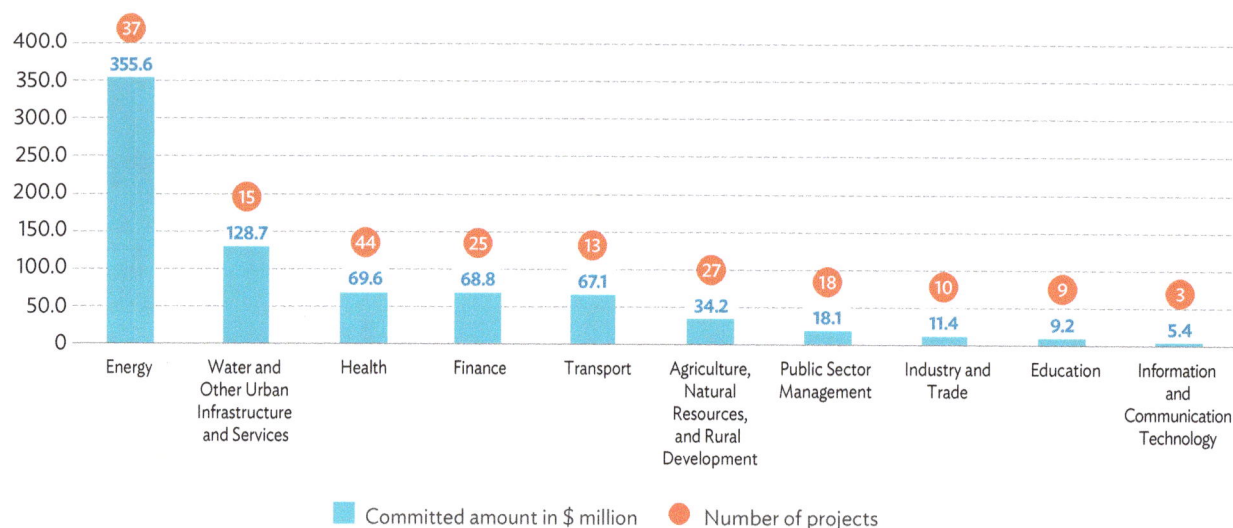

Sources: Cofinancing Database and Statement of the Asian Development Bank's Operations in 2020.

Trust Funds

The Energy sector received the most assistance from trust funds in both number and volume at 31 projects amounting to $305.3 million. This is significantly higher compared to other sectors. Water and Other Urban Infrastructure and Services received the second largest assistance at $99.8 million for 13 projects.

Figure 10: Distribution of Assistance by Sector—Trust Funds

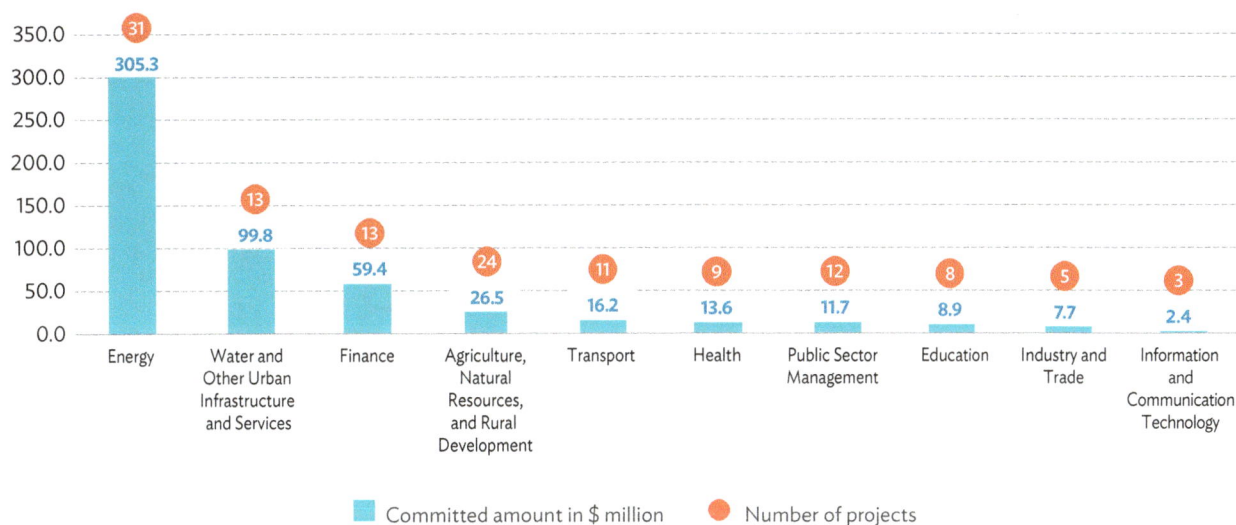

Sector	Committed amount in $ million	Number of projects
Energy	305.3	31
Water and Other Urban Infrastructure and Services	99.8	13
Finance	59.4	13
Agriculture, Natural Resources, and Rural Development	26.5	24
Transport	16.2	11
Health	13.6	9
Public Sector Management	11.7	12
Education	8.9	8
Industry and Trade	7.7	5
Information and Communication Technology	2.4	3

Source: Cofinancing Database.

Global Funds

Consistent with trust funds, Energy sector is the top sector for global funds in terms of number of commitments. In terms of amount, Transport sector received the highest committed amount at $49.0 million or 36% of total commitments.

Figure 11: Distribution of Assistance by Sector—Global Funds

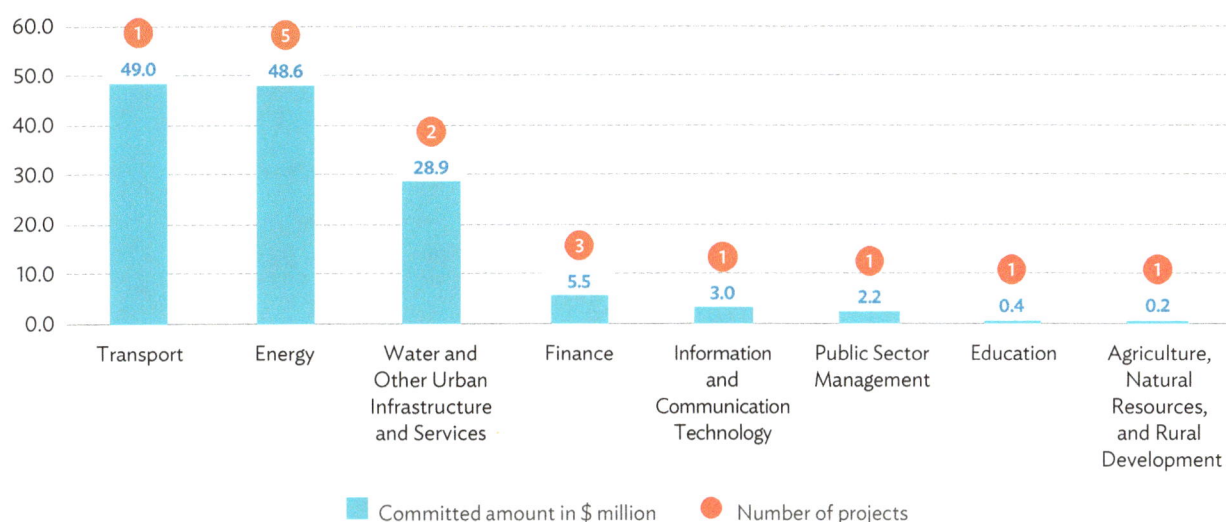

Sector	Committed amount in $ million	Number of projects
Transport	49.0	1
Energy	48.6	5
Water and Other Urban Infrastructure and Services	28.9	2
Finance	5.5	3
Information and Communication Technology	3.0	1
Public Sector Management	2.2	1
Education	0.4	1
Agriculture, Natural Resources, and Rural Development	0.2	1

Source: Cofinancing Database.

Special Funds

The Health sector received the biggest support in both volume and number of projects, with total amount of $56 million for 36 projects, of which 99% were financed by the Asia Pacific Disaster Response Fund. The Agriculture, Natural Resources, and Rural Development ($7.5 million) and the Public Sector Management ($4.3 million) sectors also received significant support from special funds. Finance (9 projects) and Agriculture, Natural Resources, and Rural Development (7) sectors recorded the second and third largest number of projects supported by Special Funds in 2020.

Figure 12: Distribution of Assistance by Sector—Special Funds

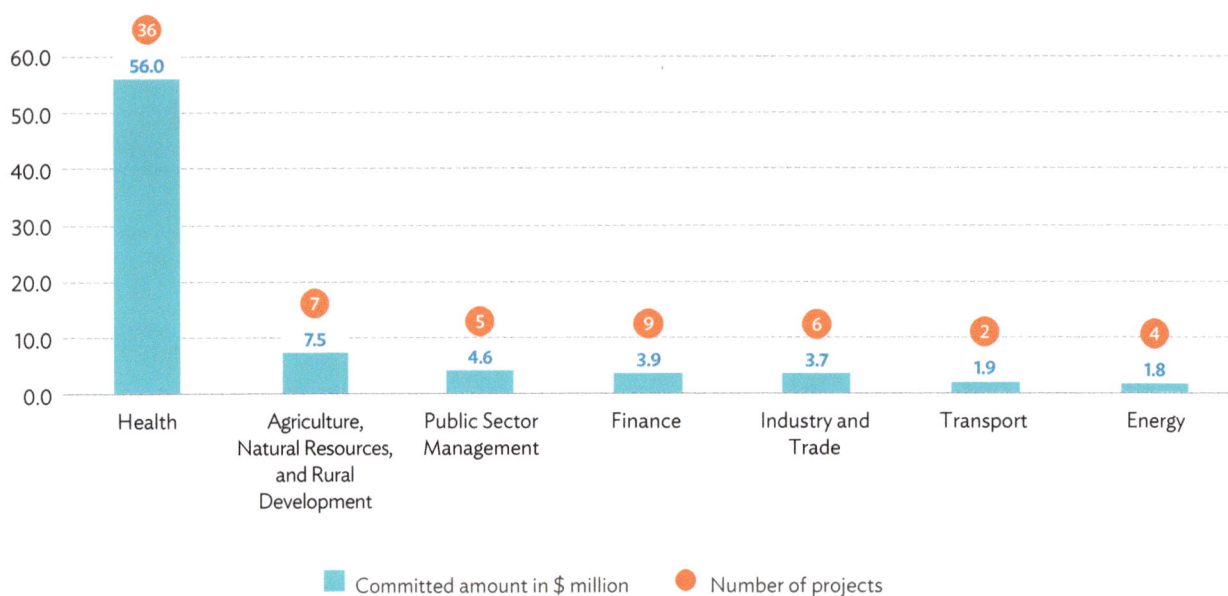

Source: Statement of the Asian Development Bank's Operations in 2020.

By Type of Assistance

Trust Funds, Global Funds, and Special Funds

Of the total 233 projects and direct charges supported in 2020, 54% are TA, 13% are direct charges, and the remaining 32% represents loans, investment grants, and equity.

Figure 13: Distribution by Type of Assistance (Count)

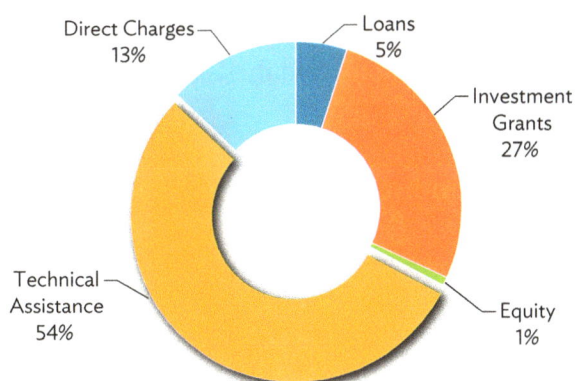

Product Type	No.
Loans	11
Investment Grants	63
Equity	2
Technical Assistance	126
Direct Charges	32
Total	**233**

Note: Count for product type may be counted twice based on modality.

Sources: Cofinancing Database and Statement of the Asian Development Bank's Operations in 2020.

A majority of commitments are for loans ($286.3 million) and investment grants ($285.7 million) each with a share of 37% of total project commitments, followed by TA at 19% ($143.5 million).

Figure 14: Distribution by Type of Assistance (Amount)
($ million)

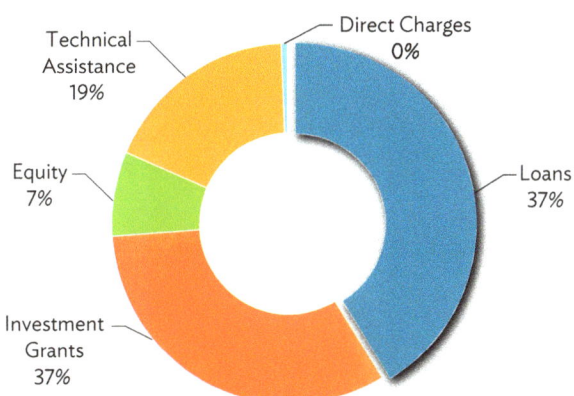

Product Type	Amount
Loans	286.3
Investment Grants	285.7
Equity	52.5
Technical Assistance	143.5
Direct Charges	4.1
Total	**772.1**

Sources: Cofinancing Database and Statement of the Asian Development Bank's Operations in 2020.

D.   TOP FUND SOURCES

Investment Projects

About 81% or $624.4 million of 2020 project and TA commitments from trust funds, global funds, and special funds financed investment projects. Of this amount, $338.9 million are for loans and equities (13 projects). The top three sources of loan and equity financing are the Leading Asia's Private Infrastructure Fund ($249.4 million), the Clean Technology Fund ($39.8 million), and the Green Climate Fund ($37.2 million).

A total of $285.7 million of trust fund, global fund, and special funds financing supported investment grants (63 projects), of which the biggest sources are the Afghanistan Infrastructure Trust Fund ($118.0 million), the Asia Pacific Disaster Response Fund ($59.6 million), and the Green Climate Fund ($40.4 million).

Figure 15: Top Fund Sources—Investment Projects

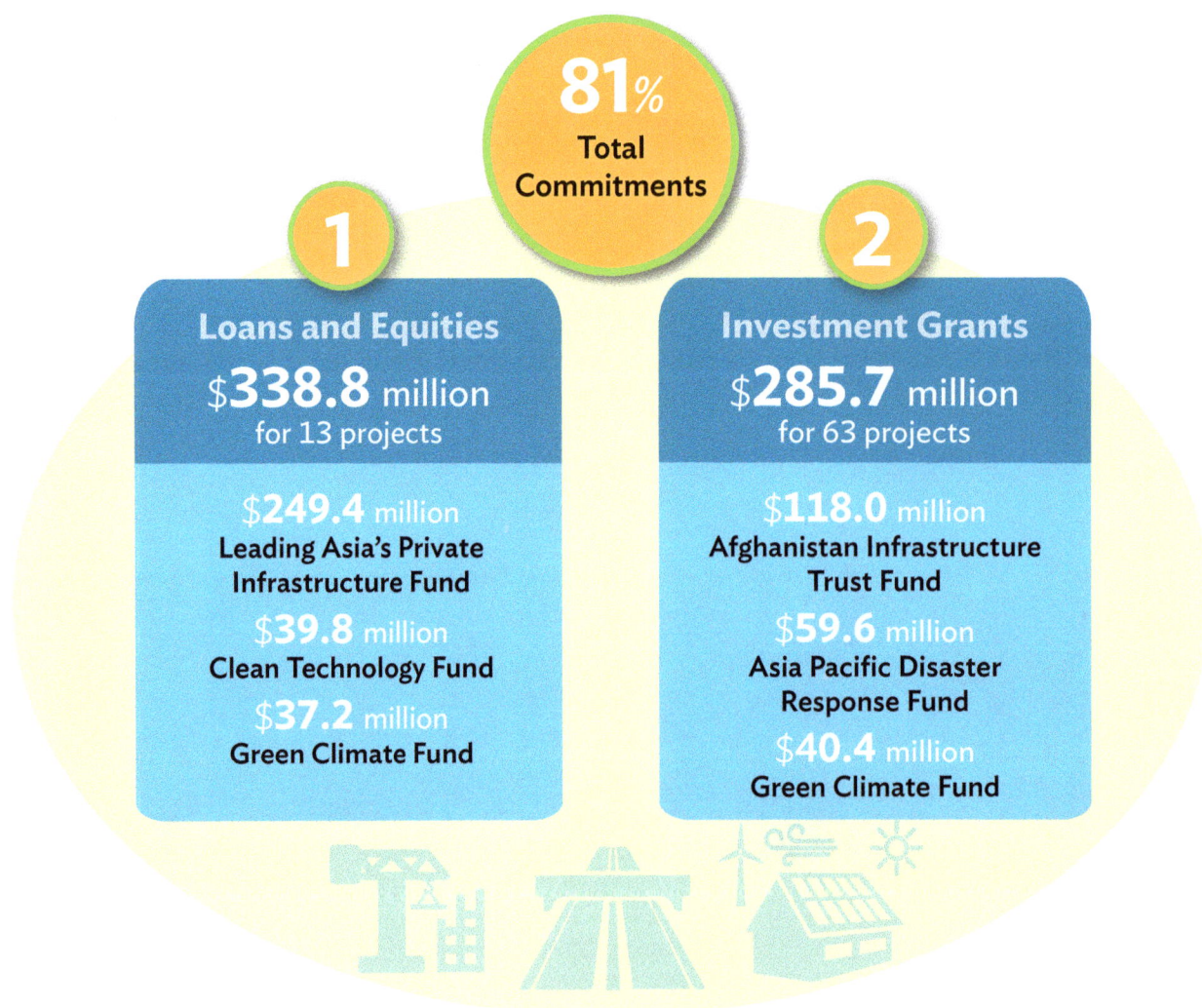

81%
Total Commitments

1

Loans and Equities
$338.8 million
for 13 projects

$249.4 million
Leading Asia's Private Infrastructure Fund

$39.8 million
Clean Technology Fund

$37.2 million
Green Climate Fund

2

Investment Grants
$285.7 million
for 63 projects

$118.0 million
Afghanistan Infrastructure Trust Fund

$59.6 million
Asia Pacific Disaster Response Fund

$40.4 million
Green Climate Fund

Sources: Cofinancing Database and Statement of the Asian Development Bank's Operations in 2020.

Technical Assistance

The Japan Fund for Poverty Reduction provided the highest TA support—$36.8 million or about 30% of the total committed amount. The Republic of Korea e-Asia and Knowledge Partnership Fund ($15 million) provided the next highest amount for TA support, while the High-Level Technology Fund ($10.8 million) the third highest.

Figure 16: Top 10 Fund Sources—Technical Assistance

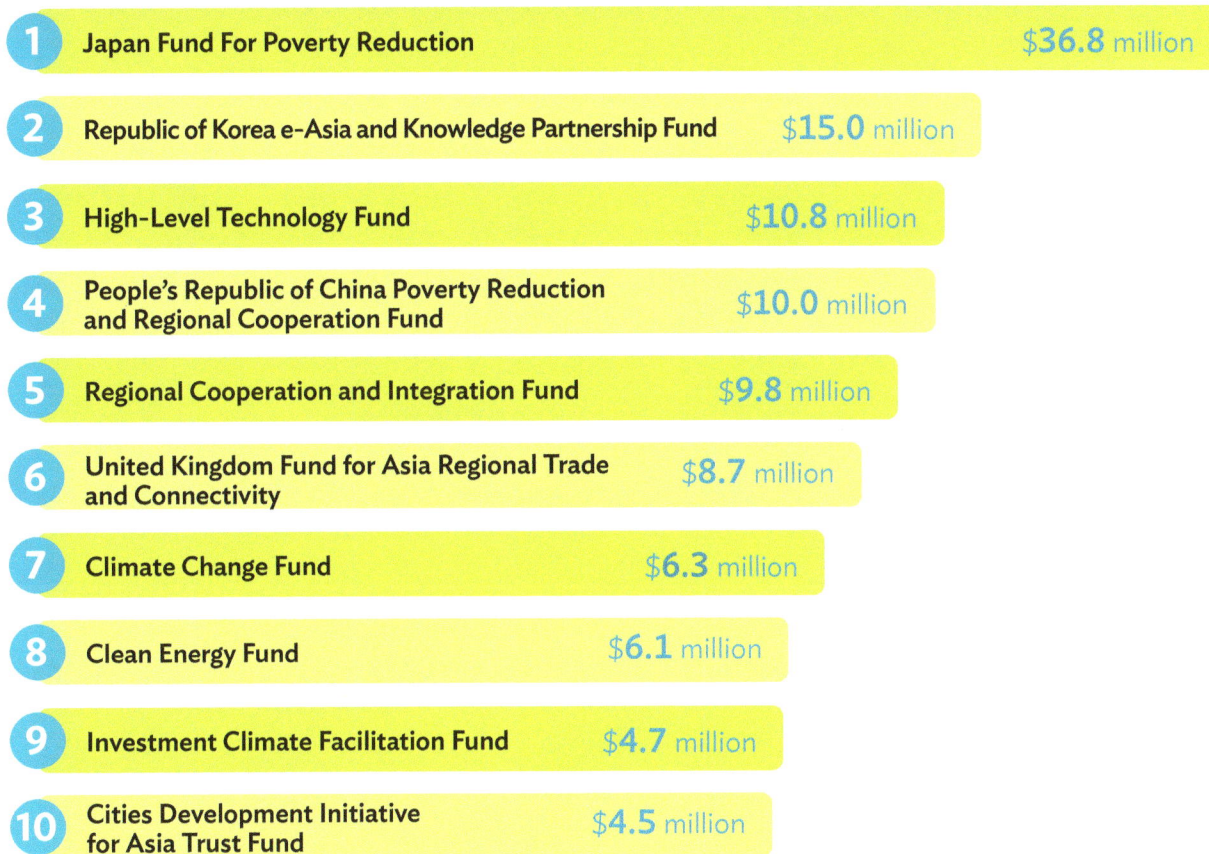

1. Japan Fund For Poverty Reduction — $36.8 million
2. Republic of Korea e-Asia and Knowledge Partnership Fund — $15.0 million
3. High-Level Technology Fund — $10.8 million
4. People's Republic of China Poverty Reduction and Regional Cooperation Fund — $10.0 million
5. Regional Cooperation and Integration Fund — $9.8 million
6. United Kingdom Fund for Asia Regional Trade and Connectivity — $8.7 million
7. Climate Change Fund — $6.3 million
8. Clean Energy Fund — $6.1 million
9. Investment Climate Facilitation Fund — $4.7 million
10. Cities Development Initiative for Asia Trust Fund — $4.5 million

Sources: Cofinancing Database and Statement of the Asian Development Bank's Operations in 2020.

E. COVID-19 RESPONSE SUPPORT

Total project commitments supporting COVID-19 response and/or recovery activities amounted to $79.3 million for 57 projects. This represents about 10.3% of total 2020 project and TA commitments from trust fund, global fund, and special fund sources. $56.2 million or 71% of COVID-19 financing came from special funds—$55.5 million from the Asia Pacific Disaster Response Fund and $0.75 million from the Regional Cooperation and Integration Fund.

Figure 17: 2020 Total and COVID-19 Project and Technical Assistance Commitments

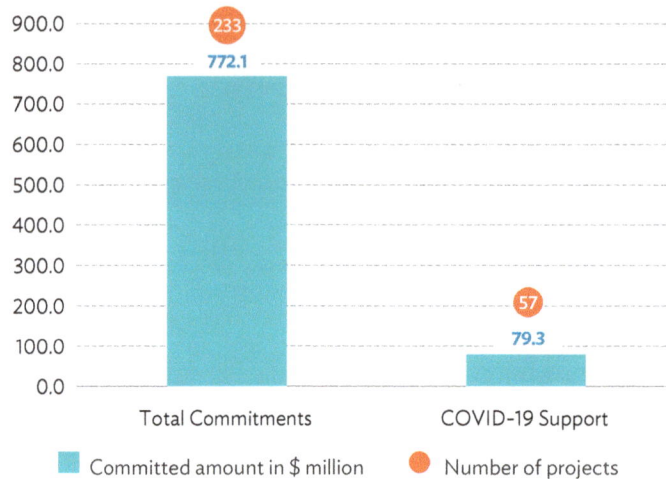

COVID-19 = coronavirus disease.
Source: Statement of the Asian Development Bank's Operations in 2020.

Figure 18: 2020 COVID-19 Support from Trust Funds, Global Funds, and Special Funds

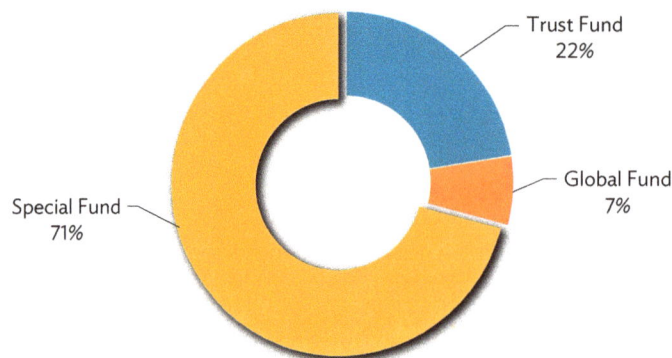

(amounts in $ million)

Source	Investment Project	TA	Total
Trust Fund	**1.3**	**16.6**	**17.9**
Japan Fund for Poverty Reduction	1.3	7.9	9.2

continued on next page

Figure 18 *continued*

Source	Investment Project	TA	Total
Republic of Korea e-Asia and Knowledge Partnership Fund	–	3.6	3.6
People's Republic of China Poverty Reduction and Regional Cooperation Fund	–	2.4	2.4
Ireland Trust Fund for Building Climate Change and Disaster Resilience in Small Island Developing States	–	1.3	1.3
High-Level Technology Fund	–	0.8	0.8
United Kingdom Fund for Asia Regional Trade and Connectivity	–	0.3	0.3
Clean Energy Fund	–	0.2	0.2
Water Financing Partnership Facility (Netherlands)	–	0.1	0.1
Gender and Development Cooperation Fund	–	0.1	0.1
Global Funds	**5.0**	**0.2**	**5.2**
Women Entrepreneurs Finance Initiative	5.0	–	5.0
Climate Investment Fund	–	0.2	0.2
Special Fund	**55.5**	**0.8**	**56.2**
Asia Pacific Disaster Response Fund	55.5	–	55.5
Regional Cooperation and Integration Fund	–	0.8	0.8
Total	**61.7**	**17.6**	**79.3**

COVID-19 = coronavirus disease, TA = technical assistance.
Source: Statement of the Asian Development Bank's Operations in 2020.

F.   NET AVAILABLE BALANCE

Total net available balance as of 31 December 2020 is $687.3 million, of which $476.8 million is available for allocation to new projects and activities in 2020. Details of net available balance by fund status and usage are shown in Table 2.

Table 2: Net Available Balance by Fund Status and Usage
($ million)

Funds with Balance for New Projects and Activities	Amount
For all departments' projects and activities	476.8
For Afghanistan projects	195.0
For scholarship program	3.1
For certified emission reduction	12.4
Total	**687.3**

Note: The funds available under the Afghanistan Infrastructure Trust Fund for Afghanistan are already marked for two projects:
(i) $143.80 million from the Afghanistan National Army Trust Fund ($45.00 million), the United States Agency for International Development ($18.00 million), and German development cooperation through Kreditanstalt für Wiederaufbau ($80.77 million) for the Energy Sector Stand Alone Project which is firm for 2021; and
(ii) $46.00 million from the Government of Japan for Transport Network Improvement Project (Kabul–Jalalabad Road) which is firm for 2022.
Sources: Trust fund, global fund, and special fund Fund Manager teams.

A total of $440.1 million or 64% of the total net available balance represents five funds with the largest balances.

Table 3: Funds with Largest Available Balance
($ million)

Fund Name	Amount
Afghanistan Infrastructure Trust Fund	195.0
Japan Fund for Poverty Reduction	131.6
Asia Pacific Disaster Response Fund	41.3
Japan Fund for the Joint Crediting Mechanism	38.6
Republic of Korea e-Asia and Knowledge Partnership Fund	33.6
Total	**440.1**

Sources: Trust fund, global fund, and special fund Fund Manager teams.

See Appendix 2 for net available balance by fund.

Inactive Funds

Nine funds are inactive and are awaiting (i) financial completion of supported projects and compliance with partner's reporting requirements, and/or (ii) receipt of instructions from partner on treatment of unutilized balances. These funds are in the process of winding down and will be closed in the near term.

Table 4: Inactive Funds

Fund Name
Australian Technical Assistance Grant
Canadian Cooperation Fund on Climate Change
Danish Cooperation Fund for Renewable Energy and Energy Efficiency in Rural Areas
Second Danish Cooperation Fund for Renewable Energy and Energy Efficiency in Rural Areas
Financial Sector Development Partnership Fund
Gender and Development Cooperation Fund
Governance Cooperation Fund
Japan Fund for Public Policy Training
Japan Special Fund

Sources: Trust fund, global fund, and special fund Fund Manager teams.

Funds Replenishment

Funds are replenished based on discussion with partners while special funds are also replenished by ADB from allocation of the net income of ADB's ordinary capital resources. Nine funds have been regularly replenished by partners for the past 3 years (Table 5).

Table 5: Funds with Regular Replenishments from External Partners, 2018–2020

Clean Energy Financing Partnership Facility
Clean Energy Fund
Stand-Alone Trust Funds
Cooperation Fund for Project Preparation in the Greater Mekong Subregion and in Other Specific Asian Countries
Domestic Resource Mobilization Trust Fund
High-Level Technology Fund
Japan Fund for Poverty Reduction
Japan Fund for the Joint Crediting Mechanism
Japan Scholarship Program
Republic of Korea e-Asia and Knowledge Partnership Fund
Special Fund
Financial Sector Development Partnership Special Fund

Source: Cofinance Management System.

As of the end of 2020, eight funds have less than $1 million available balance for new projects and activities (Table 6).

Table 6: Funds with Less than $1 Million Net Available Balance
($ million)

Fund Name	Amount
Clean Energy Financing Partnership Facility	
Asian Clean Energy Fund	0.5
Health Financing Partnership Facility	
Regional Malaria and Other Communicable Disease Threats Trust Fund	0.7
Water Financing Partnership Facility	
Sanitation Financing Partnership Trust Fund	0.4
Water Financing Partnership Facility (Multi-Donor Trust Fund)	0.8
Urban Financing Partnership Facility	
Urban Environmental Infrastructure Fund	0.5

continued on next page

Table 6 *continued*

Fund Name	Amount
Single-Partner Trust Funds	
Japan Fund for Information and Communication Technology	0.6
Multi-Partner Trust Funds	
Cooperation Fund for Regional Trade and Financial Security Initiative	0.2
Project Readiness Improvement Trust Fund	0.2

Sources: Trust fund, global fund, and special fund Fund Manager teams.

G. SUPPORT TO STRATEGY 2030 OPERATIONAL PRIORITIES

To achieve Strategy 2030's vision, ADB will focus on seven operational priority (OP) areas. Each OP will have its own operational plan, which will contribute to ADB's vision to achieve prosperity, inclusion, resilience, and sustainability.

To engender cohesion and strategic alignment in corporate performance management, results framework indicators were proposed to be consistent with corporate documents that make up the subsequent tiers of ADB's results framework architecture, such as the 2030 operational priority plans.

Out of 201 investment projects and TA supported by trust funds, global funds, and special funds in 2020, 167 committed projects have classification to the operational priorities. Project teams identified the proper OP classification on the basis of a tagging methodology issued by the Strategy, Policy, and Partnerships Department. Classification commenced beginning in April 2019 ADB-approved projects, except for (i) supplementary approvals for additional financing, and (ii) Private Sector Operations Department (PSOD) loans and equities. (See Appendix 3 for the list of committed projects ssupporting OPs.)

Of the seven OPs, OP1: Addressing remaining poverty and reducing inequalities (83%), OP6: Strengthening governance and institutional capacity (77%), and OP2: Accelerating progress in gender equality (70%) were the most supported operational priorities by projects committed in 2020.

Seven Operational Priorities of ADB Strategy 2030

OP 1	OP 2	OP 3	OP 4	OP 5	OP 6	OP 7
Addressing remaining poverty and reducing inequalities	Accelerating progress in gender equality	Tackling climate change, building climate and disaster resilience, and enhancing environmental sustainability	Making cities more livable	Promoting rural development and food security	Strengthening governance and institutional capacity	Fostering regional cooperation and integration

Figure 19 shows the classification of total 2020 trust fund, global fund, and special fund-supported projects according to operational priorities. Table 7 provides the summary of support by fund to the seven operational priorities.

Figure 19: Classification of 2020 Committed Projects According to Strategy 2030 Operational Priorities (%)

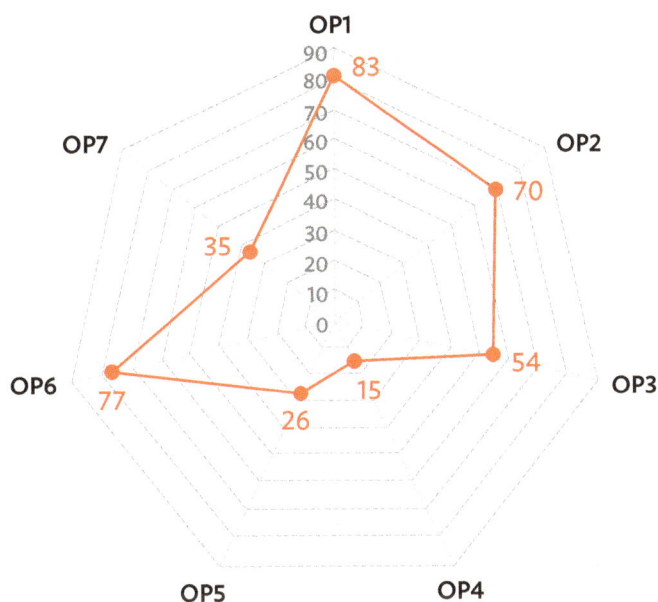

OP = operational priority.
Source: eOperations.

Table 7: 2020 Funds Support to Strategy 2030 Operational Priorities

Fund Name	Project Count	OP 1	OP 2	OP 3	OP 4	OP 5	OP 6	OP 7
Afghanistan Infrastructure Trust Fund	2	2	2	2	0	1	1	2
Asia Pacific Climate Finance Fund	2	2	2	2	1	1	2	2
Asia Pacific Disaster Response Fund	39	38	2	9	1	3	17	0
Asian Clean Energy Fund	3	1	3	3	0	1	3	1
Canadian Climate Fund for the Private Sector in Asia	1	1	1	1	0	1	1	1
Canadian Climate Fund for the Private Sector in Asia II	2	0	0	0	0	0	0	0
Cities Development Initiative for Asia Trust Fund	1	1	1	1	1	1	1	1
Clean Energy Fund	9	6	7	7	2	2	7	3
Clean Technology Fund	4	2	3	3	2	2	3	2

continued on next page

Table 7 *continued*

Fund Name	Project Count	OP 1	OP 2	OP 3	OP 4	OP 5	OP 6	OP 7
Climate Change Fund	8	4	5	6	1	2	4	3
Cooperation Fund for Project Preparation in the Greater Mekong Subregion and in Other Specific Asian Countries	1	1	1	1	1	0	1	1
Financial Sector Development Partnership Special Fund	9	8	8	5	0	1	8	2
Gender and Development Cooperation Fund	1	1	1	1	1	0	1	0
Global Environment Facility	1	1	1	1	1	1	1	1
Global Partnership for Education Fund	1	0	0	0	0	0	0	0
Green Climate Fund	2	2	2	2	2	1	2	1
High-Level Technology Fund	18	10	9	8	3	5	7	4
Integrated Disaster Risk Management Fund	2	0	1	1	0	0	1	0
Investment Climate Facilitation Fund	3	0	1	1	0	0	3	3
Ireland Trust Fund for Building Climate Change and Disaster Resilience in Small Island Developing States	3	2	2	2	0	0	2	2
Japan Fund for Information and Communication Technology	1	1	1	0	0	0	1	0
Japan Fund for Poverty Reduction	34	30	32	21	8	17	29	10
Japan Fund for the Joint Crediting Mechanism	1	1	1	1	1	0	1	0
Leading Asia's Private Infrastructure Fund	8	0	0	0	0	0	0	0
People's Republic of China Poverty Reduction and Regional Cooperation Fund	13	8	11	8	1	3	13	11
Regional Cooperation and Integration Fund	14	8	11	8	0	2	11	13
Republic of Korea e-Asia and Knowledge Partnership Fund	25	14	17	8	5	3	21	12
Sanitation Financing Partnership Trust Fund	2	2	2	2	1	2	2	2
Strategic Climate Fund	4	3	4	3	0	1	3	0
United Kingdom Fund for Asia Regional Trade and Connectivity	6	2	3	1	0	0	3	4
Urban Climate Change Resilience Trust Fund	3	3	3	3	2	1	3	1
Water Financing Partnership Facility (Multi-Donor Trust Fund)	1	1	1	1	0	1	1	1
Water Financing Partnership Facility (Netherlands)	7	4	4	4	0	4	4	0
Women Entrepreneurs Finance Initiative	3	3	3	0	0	0	1	0
Total	**201**	**138**	**117**	**91**	**25**	**43**	**128**	**59**

OP = operational priority.
Source: eOperations.

Figure 20: 2020 Committed Projects Support to Strategy 2030 Operational Priorities

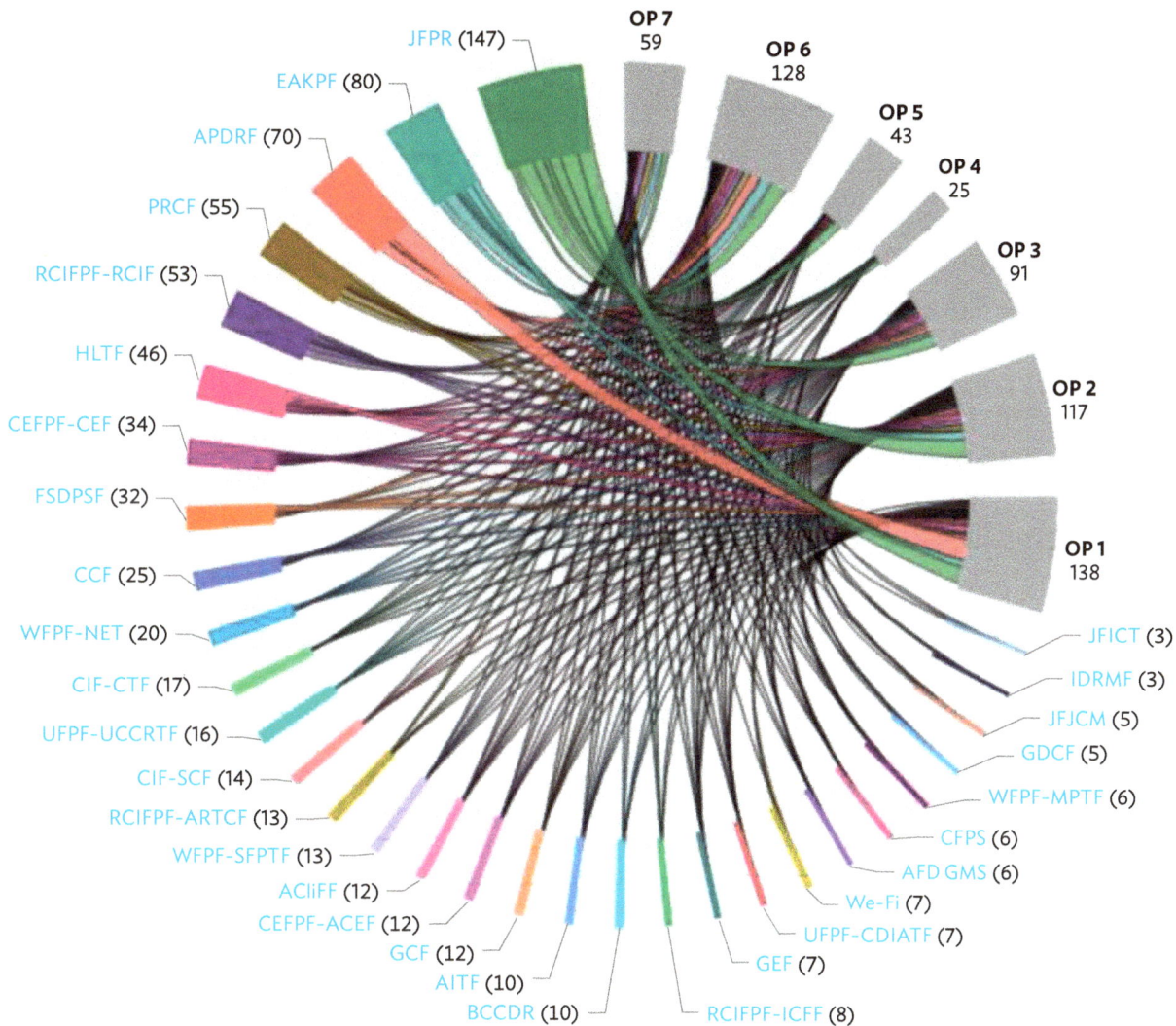

ACliFF = Asia Pacific Climate Finance Fund, AFD GMS = Cooperation Fund for Project Preparation in the Greater Mekong Subregion and in Other Specific Asian Countries, AITF = Afghanistan Infrastructure Trust Fund, APDRF = Asia Pacific Disaster Response Fund, BCCDR = Ireland Trust Fund for Building Climate Change and Disaster Resilience in Small Island Developing States, CCF = Climate Change Fund, CEFPF-ACEF = Asian Clean Energy Fund under the Clean Energy Financing Partnership Facility, CEFPF-CEF = Clean Energy Fund under the Clean Energy Financing Partnership Facility, CFPS = Canadian Climate Fund for the Private Sector in Asia under the Clean Energy Financing Partnership Facility, CIF-CTF = Clean Technology Fund under the Climate Investment Fund, CIF-SCF = Strategic Climate Fund under the Climate Investment Fund, EAKPF = Republic of Korea e-Asia and Knowledge Partnership Fund, FSDPSF = Financial Sector Development Partnership Special Fund, GCF = Green Climate Fund, GDCF = Gender and Development Cooperation Fund, GEF = Global Environment Facility, HLTF = High-Level Technology Fund, IDRMF = Integrated Disaster Risk Management Fund, JFICT = Japan Fund for Information and Communication Technology, JFJCM = Japan Fund for the Joint Crediting Mechanism, JFPR = Japan Fund for Poverty Reduction, OP = operational priority, PRCF = People's Republic of China Poverty Reduction and Regional Cooperation Fund, RCIFPF-ARTCF = United Kingdom Fund for Asia Regional Trade and Connectivity under the Regional Cooperation and Integration Financing Partnership Facility, RCIFPF-ICFF = Investment Climate Facilitation Fund under the Regional Cooperation and Integration Financing Partnership Facility, RCIFPF-RCIF = Regional Cooperation and Integration Fund under the Regional Cooperation and Integration Financing Partnership Facility, UFPF-CDIATF = Cities Development Initiative for Asia Trust Fund under the Urban Financing Partnership Facility, UFPF-UCCRTF = Urban Climate Change Resilience Trust Fund under the Urban Financing Partnership Facility, We-Fi = Women Entrepreneurs Finance Initiative, WFPF-MPTF = Multi-Donor Trust Fund under the Water Financing Partnership Facility, WFPF-NET = Netherlands Trust Fund under the Water Financing Partnership Facility, WFPF-SFPTF = Sanitation Financing Partnership Trust Fund under the Water Financing Partnership Facility.

Note: Figure indicated in each fund refers to total count of OP tags (OP1 to OP7) and not the actual number of projects supported by the funds in 2020.

Source: OP tags from eOperations.

APPENDIXES

2020 Contributions from External Partners
($ million)

Fund Name	Partner	2020 Contributions		
Trust Funds		Original Currency	Amount in Original Currency	USD Equivalent
Clean Energy Fund	Norway	NOK	2.0	0.2
	United Kingdom	GBP	0.5	0.6
Domestic Resource Mobilization Trust Fund	Japan	USD	1.4	1.4
Japan Fund for the Joint Crediting Mechanism	Japan	JPY	1,000.0	9.3
Republic of Korea e-Asia and Knowledge Partnership Fund	Korea, Republic of	KRW	9,231.0	8.4
Cooperation Fund for Project Preparation in the Greater Mekong Subregion and in Other Specific Asian Countries	France	EUR	1.0	1.1
Japan Fund for Poverty Reduction	Japan	JPY	2,717.0	24.7
	Japan	JPY	7,904.8	73.8
High-Level Technology Fund	Japan	JPY	1,650.0	15.8
Japan Scholarship Program	Japan	USD	5.0	5.0
Regional Malaria and Other Communicable Disease Threats Trust Fund	United Kingdom	GBP	4.8	6.5
Canadian Climate Fund for the Private Sector in Asia II	Canada	CAD	30.0	22.6
Leading Asia's Private Sector Infrastructure Fund	Japan	USD	83.3	83.3
	Japan	USD	17.0	17.0
Afghanistan Infrastructure Trust Fund	Canada	USD	1.6	1.6
	ANA Trust Fund	USD	25.0	25.0
ADB Ventures Investment Fund 1	Clean Technology Fund	USD	13.0	13.0
	Nordic Development Fund	EUR	9.0	9.8
	Korea, Republic of	USD	5.0	5.0
	Korea Venture Investment Corporation	USD	10.0	10.0
	Finland	EUR	20.0	21.8
ADB Ventures Investment Fund 2	Clean Technology Fund	USD	4.0	4.0

continued on next page

Appendix 1 *continued*

Fund Name	Partner	2020 Contributions		
Australian Climate Finance Partnership	Australia	AUD	140.0	106.0
Trust Funds				**466.1**
Global Funds (net of cancellations)				
Global Environment Facility				3.0
Green Climate Fund				78.6
Global Partnership for Education				0.4
Climate Investment Funds				72.6
Global Agriculture and Food Security Program				4.0
Global Funds				**158.6**
Special Funds				
Financial Sector Development Partnership Special Fund	Luxembourg	EUR	1.7	2.0
Asia Pacific Disaster Response Fund	Japan	USD	75.0	75.0
Special Funds				77.0
Total				**701.8**

AUD = Australian dollar, CAD = Canadian dollar, EUR = euro, GBP = pound sterling, JPY = yen, KRW = won, NOK = Norwegian krone, USD = United States dollar.

Notes:
1. Excludes 2020 ADB's allocation from ordinary capital resources net income to special funds.
2. Contribution received from Japan for the Leading Asia's Private Sector Infrastructure Fund or LEAP ($100.3 million) and the Canadian Climate Fund for the Private Sector in Asia II ($22.6 million) is part of partner's commitment (LEAP: $1.5 billion, CFPS II: $149.4 million); Controller's Department formally recognized and recorded in ADB's system and financial statements once they are remitted by the financing partner to ADB.

Source: Cofinance Management System.

Breakdown of Available Balance by Status, 31 December 2020 ($ million)

Funds with Balances for New Projects and Activities	Net Available Balance
Clean Energy Financing Partnership Facility	**42.9**
Carbon Capture and Storage Fund	12.2
Clean Energy Fund	27.5
Canadian Climate Fund for the Private Sector in Asia	2.7
Asian Clean Energy Fund	0.5
Health Financing Partnership Facility	**0.7**
Regional Malaria and Other Communicable Disease Threats Trust Fund	0.7
Regional Cooperation and Integration Financing Partnership Facility (RCIFPF)	**9.5**
Investment Climate Facilitation Fund	3.2
United Kingdom Fund for Asia Regional Trade and Connectivity	6.3
Urban Financing Partnership Facility	**26.5**
Urban Climate Change Resilience Trust Fund	20.8
Urban Environmental Infrastructure Fund	0.5
Cities Development in Asia Trust Fund	1.4
ASEAN Australia Smart Cities Fund	3.9
Water Financing Partnership Facility	**2.9**
Sanitation Financing Partnership Trust Fund	0.4
Netherlands Trust Fund	1.7
Multi-Donor Trust Fund	0.8
ADB Ventures Financing Partner Facility	
ADB Ventures Investment Fund 1[a]	–
Single-Partner Trust Funds	**242.7**
Japan Fund for Poverty Reduction	131.6
Republic of Korea e-Asia and Knowledge Partnership Fund	33.6
Japan Fund for the Joint Crediting Mechanism	38.6
People's Republic of China Poverty Reduction and Regional Cooperation Fund	24.9
Japan Fund for Information and Communication Technology	0.6
Cooperation Fund for Project Preparation in the Greater Mekong Subregion and in Other Specific Asian Countries	2.0

continued on next page

Funds with Balances for New Projects and Activities	Net Available Balance
Spanish Cooperation Fund for Technical Assistance	4.0
Japan Fund for Public Policy Training	7.5
Multi-Partner Trust Funds	**61.7**
Cooperation Fund for Regional Trade and Financial Security Initiative	0.2
Asia Pacific Project Preparation Facility	30.9
Project Readiness Improvement Trust Fund	0.2
High-Level Technology Fund	17.8
Asia Pacific Climate Finance Fund	9.3
Domestic Resource Mobilization Trust Fund	3.2
Special Funds	**90.0**
Asia Pacific Disaster Response Fund	41.3
Climate Change Fund	21.4
Financial Sector Development Partnership Special Fund	2.1
Regional Cooperation and Integration Fund (under RCIFPF)	25.2
Funds with Balances for Specific Usage	**210.5**
Australian Climate Finance Partnership[a]	–
Canadian Climate Fund for Private Sector in Asia II[a]	–
Leading Asia's Private Sector Infrastructure Fund[a]	–
Japan Scholarship Program	3.1
Afghanistan Infrastructure Trust Fund	195.0
Future Carbon Fund	12.4
Total	**687.3**

ASEAN= Association of Southeast Asian Nations.
[a] Net available balance is commercially sensitive information and cannot be disclosed to the public.
Source: Fund Manager Teams.

2020 Committed Projects with Operational Priorities Classification ($ million)

Fund Name/ RD	Product Type	Product Approval Number	DMC	Project Title	ADB Approved Amount	Approval Date	Signing Date	OP1	OP2	OP3	OP4	OP5	OP6	OP7
Afghanistan Infrastructure Trust Fund														
CWRD	Grant	0770	AFG	Energy Supply Improvement Investment Program—Tranche 7	118.00	2-Dec-2020	18-Dec-2020	✓	✓	✓				✓
CWRD	TA	6664	AFG	Natural Resources Operations Support and Enhancement	1.56	9-Dec-2020	15-Dec-2020	✓	✓	✓		✓	✓	✓
Asia Pacific Climate Finance Fund														
PSOD	TA	9948	REG	ADB Ventures Technical Assistance (Supplementary)	1.40	29-Sep-2020	29-Sep-2020	✓	✓	✓	✓	✓	✓	✓
SERD	TA	9766	REG	Southeast Asia Public Management, Financial Sector, and Trade Policy Facility (Supplementary)	2.50	10-Dec-2020	10-Dec-2020	✓	✓	✓			✓	✓
Asia Pacific Disaster Response Fund														
CWRD	Grant	0729	ARM	COVID-19 Emergency Response	2.00	3-Aug-2020	27-Aug-2020	✓					✓	
CWRD	Grant	0773	GEO	COVID-19 Emergency Response	2.50	3-Dec-2020	30-Dec-2020	✓		✓			✓	
CWRD	Grant	0735	KAZ	COVID-19 Emergency Response	3.00	27-Aug-2020	15-Dec-2020	✓					✓	
CWRD	Grant	0694	PAK	COVID-19 Emergency Response	2.00	30-Mar-2020	3-Nov-2020	✓					✓	
CWRD	Grant	0730	TAJ	COVID-19 Emergency Response	2.50	5-Aug-2020	17-Sep-2020	✓					✓	
CWRD	Grant	0738	UZB	COVID-19 Emergency Response	3.00	14-Sep-2020	16-Oct-2020	✓					✓	
EARD	Grant	0688	MON	COVID-19 Emergency Response	1.00	25-Mar-2020	26-Mar-2020	✓					✓	
EARD	Grant	0734	MON	COVID-19 Emergency Response (Phase 2)	1.50	3-Sep-2020	15-Sep-2020	✓					✓	
PARD	Grant	0725	COO	COVID-19 Emergency Response	1.00	29-Jul-2020	5-Aug-2020	✓						
PARD	Grant	0744	FIJ	COVID-19 Emergency Response	2.00	2-Oct-2020	27-Nov-2020	✓						
PARD	Grant	0697	FIJ	Tropical Cyclone Harold Emergency Response	0.40	28-Apr-2020	7-May-2020	✓		✓			✓	
PARD	Grant	0691	FSM	COVID-19 Emergency Response	0.47	31-Mar-2020	7-Apr-2020	✓						

continued on next page

Fund Name/RD	Product Type	Product Approval Number	DMC	Project Title	ADB Approved Amount	Approval Date	Signing Date	OP1	OP2	OP3	OP4	OP5	OP6	OP7
PARD	Grant	0722	FSM	COVID-19 Emergency Response	1.03	29-Jul-2020	7-Aug-2020	✓						
PARD	Grant	0723	KIR	COVID-19 Emergency Response	1.50	29-Jul-2020	31-Aug-2020	✓						
PARD	Grant	0689	NAU	COVID-19 Emergency Response	0.32	31-Mar-2020	9-Apr-2020	✓						
PARD	Grant	0745	NAU	COVID-19 Emergency Response	0.68	2-Oct-2020	16-Oct-2020	✓						
PARD	Grant	0743	NIU	COVID-19 Emergency Response	0.50	2-Oct-2020	22-Oct-2020	✓						
PARD	Grant	0727	PAL	COVID-19 Emergency Response	1.00	29-Jul-2020	4-Aug-2020	✓						
PARD	Grant	0719	PNG	COVID-19 Emergency Response	3.00	29-Jul-2020	5-Aug-2020	✓						
PARD	Grant	0692	RMI	COVID-19 Emergency Response	0.37	31-Mar-2020	14-Apr-2020	✓						
PARD	Grant	0728	RMI	COVID-19 Emergency Response	0.63	29-Jul-2020	19-Aug-2020	✓						
PARD	Grant	0721	SAM	COVID-19 Emergency Response	1.50	29-Jul-2020	20-Aug-2020	✓						
PARD	Grant	0724	SOL	COVID-19 Emergency Response	1.50	29-Jul-2020	5-Aug-2020	✓						
PARD	Grant	0693	TON	COVID-19 Emergency Response	0.47	6-Apr-2020	8-Apr-2020	✓						
PARD	Grant	0698	TON	Tropical Cyclone Harold Emergency Response	0.20	30-Apr-2020	12-May-2020			✓			✓	
PARD	Grant	0690	TUV	COVID-19 Emergency Response	0.37	31-Mar-2020	15-Apr-2020	✓						
PARD	Grant	0726	TUV	COVID-19 Emergency Response	0.63	29-Jul-2020	5-Aug-2020	✓						
PARD	Grant	0720	VAN	COVID-19 Emergency Response	1.50	29-Jul-2020	7-Aug-2020	✓						
PARD	Grant	0695	VAN	Tropical Cyclone Harold Emergency Response	1.00	17-Apr-2020	11-May-2020	✓				✓		
SARD	Grant	0731	BAN	COVID-19 Emergency Response	3.00	5-Aug-2020	29-Sep-2020	✓	✓	✓	✓			
SARD	Grant	0715	BHU	COVID-19 Emergency Response	2.00	16-Jul-2020	22-Jul-2020	✓		✓			✓	
SARD	Grant	0687	MLD	COVID-19 Emergency Response	0.50	25-Mar-2020	26-Mar-2020	✓					✓	
SARD	Grant	0716	MLD	COVID-19 Emergency Response	1.00	16-Jul-2020	8-Aug-2020	✓		✓			✓	
SARD	Grant	0712	NEP	COVID-19 Emergency Response	3.00	29-Jun-2020	6-Jul-2020	✓		✓			✓	
SARD	Grant	0702	SRI	COVID-19 Emergency Response	3.00	2-Jun-2020	8-Jun-2020	✓		✓			✓	
SERD	Grant	0686	INO	COVID-19 Emergency Response	3.00	20-Mar-2020	1-Apr-2020	✓					✓	
SERD	Grant	0685	PHI	COVID-19 Emergency Response	3.00	13-Mar-2020	16-Mar-2020	✓					✓	
SERD	Grant	0707	TIM	COVID-19 Food Security Emergency Response	1.00	18-Jun-2020	9-Jul-2020	✓	✓			✓		
SERD	Grant	0750	VIE	Viet Nam Tropical Storms Response	2.50	6-Nov-2020	24-Nov-2020	✓		✓		✓		

continued on next page

Fund Name/ RD	Product Type	Product Approval Number	DMC	Project Title	ADB Approved Amount	Approval Date	Signing Date	OP1	OP2	OP3	OP4	OP5	OP6	OP7
Asian Clean Energy Fund														
EARD	TA	9941	MON	Supporting Renewable Energy Development Project	1.30	16-Jan-2020	11-Feb-2020		✓	✓			✓	
PARD	TA	6680	REG	Preparing Floating Solar Plus Projects under the Pacific Renewable Energy Investment Facility	2.00	15-Dec-2020	15-Dec-2020		✓	✓			✓	✓
SERD	Grant	0753	INO	Sustainable Energy Access in Eastern Indonesia — Electricity Grid Development Program (Phase 2)	3.00	24-Nov-2020	8-Dec-2020	✓	✓	✓			✓	✓
Canadian Climate Fund for the Private Sector in Asia														
PSOD	TA	9949	AFG	Herat Wind	0.23	12-Feb-2020	12-Feb-2020	✓	✓	✓		✓	✓	✓
Canadian Climate Fund for the Private Sector in Asia II														
PSOD	Loan	8370	BAN	Spectra Solar Power	4.44	29-Jul-2019	9-Jun-2020							
PSOD	Loan	8388	UZB	Navoi Solar Power	8.00	30-Sep-2020	9-Dec-2020							
Cities Development Initiative for Asia Trust Fund														
SDCC	TA	6559	REG	Implementing the Cities Development Initiative for Asia	4.50	8-Sep-2020	8-Sep-2020	✓	✓	✓	✓	✓	✓	✓
Clean Energy Fund														
CWRD	TA	6564	KAZ	Supporting Renewable Technology-Inclusive Heat Supply Legislation	1.00	14-Sep-2020	25-Sep-2020		✓	✓			✓	
CWRD	TA	6637	UZB	Promoting Distributed Solar Photovoltaic Systems for Enhanced Access to Energy	1.00	7-Dec-2020	29-Dec-2020	✓	✓	✓			✓	
EARD	TA	6560	PRC	Climate Change Financing Acceleration Platform	1.00	8-Sep-2020	3-Oct-2020	✓	✓	✓			✓	
SARD	TA	9389	SRI	Rooftop Solar Power Generation (Supplementary)	0.25	9-Jul-2020	9-Jul-2020							
SDCC	TA	9960	REG	Integrated High Impact Innovation in Sustainable Energy Technology: Pilot Testing of Innovative Energy Technologies and Business Models (Subproject 3)	0.60	1-Apr-2020	1-Apr-2020	✓	✓	✓	✓	✓	✓	✓
SDCC	TA	6619	REG	Marine Aquaculture, Reefs, Renewable Energy, and Ecotourism for Ecosystem Services	1.00	1-Dec-2020	1-Dec-2020	✓	✓	✓			✓	✓

continued on next page

Fund Name/ RD	Product Type	Product Approval Number	DMC	Project Title	ADB Approved Amount	Approval Date	Signing Date	OP1	OP2	OP3	OP4	OP5	OP6	OP7
SDCC	TA	6563	REG	Regional Support to Build Disease Resilient and Energy Efficient Centralized Air-conditioning Systems	0.50	12-Sep-2020	12-Sep-2020	✓	✓	✓	✓	✓	✓	✓
SERD	Grant	0737	CAM	Grid Reinforcement	2.00	10-Sep-2020	12-Oct-2020	✓	✓	✓			✓	
SERD	TA	9600	REG	Southeast Asia Energy Sector Development, Investment Planning, and Capacity Building Facility (Supplementary)	0.75	14-Sep-2020	14-Sep-2020							
Clean Technology Fund														
PSOD	Loan	8377	THA	Southern Thailand Wind Power and Battery Energy Storage	4.75	12-Jan-2020	15-May-2020							
PSOD	TA	9948	REG	ADB Ventures Technical Assistance (Supplementary)	3.00	31-Dec-2020	31-Dec-2020	✓	✓	✓	✓	✓	✓	✓
SDCC	TA	9960	REG	Integrated High Impact Innovation in Sustainable Energy Technology: Pilot Testing of Innovative Energy Technologies and Business Models (Subproject 3)	0.40	1-Apr-2020	1-Apr-2020	✓	✓	✓	✓	✓	✓	✓
SERD	Loan	8380	INO	Geothermal Power Generation	35.00	28-May-2020	19-Aug-2020		✓	✓			✓	
Climate Change Fund														
CWRD	TA	6663	PAK	Strengthening Food Security Post–COVID-19 and Locust Attacks	0.20	9-Dec-2020	9-Dec-2020	✓	✓	✓		✓	✓	
EARD	TA	6661	PRC	Customized Low-Carbon Development Models in Rural and Small and Medium-Sized Towns	0.75	8-Dec-2020	30-Dec-2020		✓	✓			✓	
PARD	TA	6683	REG	Support to Climate-Resilient Investment Pathways in the Pacific	1.00	15-Dec-2020	15-Dec-2020				✓			✓
SARD	TA	6598	BHU	Preparing Renewable Energy for Climate Resilience	0.25	18-Nov-2020	24-Nov-2020	✓	✓	✓				
SDCC	TA	6627	REG	Building Institutional Capacity: Delivering Climate Solutions under Operational Priority 3 of Strategy 2030	2.00	3-Dec-2020	3-Dec-2020	✓	✓	✓			✓	✓
SDCC	TA	9960	REG	Integrated High Impact Innovation in Sustainable Energy Technology - Pilot Testing of Innovative Energy Technologies and Business Models (Subproject 3)	0.30	1-Apr-2020	1-Apr-2020	✓	✓	✓	✓	✓	✓	✓
SDCC	TA	9461	REG	Protecting and Investing in Natural Capital in Asia and the Pacific (Supplementary)	0.80	28-Feb-2020	28-Feb-2020							

continued on next page

Fund Name/ RD	Product Type	Product Approval Number	DMC	Project Title	ADB Approved Amount	Approval Date	Signing Date	OP1	OP2	OP3	OP4	OP5	OP6	OP7
SERD	TA	9323	LAO	Sustainable Rural Infrastructure and Watershed Management Sector Facility (Second Supplementary)	1.00	14-Dec-2020	14-Dec-2020							
Cooperation Fund for Project Preparation in the Greater Mekong Subregion and in Other Specific Asian Countries														
SERD	TA	9225	REG	Southeast Asia Transport Project Preparatory Facility Phase 2 (Supplementary)	0.75	8-Sep-2020	8-Sep-2020	✓	✓	✓	✓		✓	✓
Financial Sector Development Partnership Special Fund														
CWRD	TA	6554	KAZ	Preparing the Green Investments Finance Project	0.23	27-Aug-2020	27-Aug-2020	✓	✓	✓			✓	
CWRD	TA	9627	KGZ	Promoting Economic Diversification Program (Third Supplementary)	0.40	24-Jul-2020	24-Jul-2020	✓	✓	✓			✓	✓
EARD	TA	6687	PRC	Supporting Sustainable Finance and Regional Cooperation	0.20	17-Dec-2020	31-Dec-2020				✓		✓	✓
PSOD	TA	6532	REG	Promoting Digital Finance Solutions for Inclusive Finance Among Partner Financial Institutions	0.50	1-Jul-2020	1-Jul-2020	✓	✓			✓	✓	
SARD	TA	6552	BAN	Capacity Development of the Bangladesh Infrastructure Finance Fund	0.65	18-Aug-2020	11-Oct-2020	✓	✓	✓			✓	
SARD	TA	6677	BHU	Capacity Building for Rural Finance Development	0.25	11-Dec-2020	15-Dec-2020	✓	✓				✓	
SARD	TA	6581	BHU	Strengthening the Financial Market Development Program	0.25	27-Oct-2020	3-Nov-2020	✓	✓				✓	
SDCC	TA	9364	REG	Strengthening Financial Sector Operations in Asia and the Pacific (Supplementary)	0.50	20-Oct-2020	20-Oct-2020	✓	✓				✓	
SERD	TA	9333	INO	Promoting Innovative Financial Inclusion (Supplementary)	0.30	12-Aug-2020	12-Aug-2020	✓	✓	✓				
Gender and Development Cooperation Fund														
SDCC	TA	9660	REG	Promoting Transformative Gender Equality Agenda in Asia and the Pacific (Supplementary)	0.11	2-Dec-2020	2-Dec-2020	✓	✓	✓	✓		✓	
Global Environment Facility														
SDCC	TA	9911	REG	Promoting Action on Plastic Pollution from Source to Sea in Asia and the Pacific–Enhancing Knowledge and Creating Enabling Environments for Reducing Marine Plastic Pollution (Subproject 1)	0.23	20-Oct-2020	20-Oct-2020	✓	✓	✓	✓	✓	✓	✓

continued on next page

Fund Name/ RD	Product Type	Product Approval Number	DMC	Project Title	ADB Approved Amount	Approval Date	Signing Date	OP1	OP2	OP3	OP4	OP5	OP6	OP7
Global Partnership for Education Fund														
PARD	TA	9645	REG	Strengthening Education in the Pacific Region (Supplementary)	0.39	10-Feb-2020	10-Feb-2020							
Green Climate Fund														
CWRD	Grant	0649	PAK	Karachi Bus Rapid Transit Red Line	11.80	5-Jul-2019	19-Jun-2020	✓	✓	✓	✓		✓	
CWRD	Loan	8367	PAK	Karachi Bus Rapid Transit Red Line	37.20	5-Jul-2019	19-Jun-2020	✓	✓	✓	✓		✓	
PARD	Grant	0653	KIR	South Tarawa Water Supply	28.63	30-Aug-2019	6-Nov-2020	✓	✓	✓	✓	✓	✓	✓
High-Level Technology Fund														
CWRD	TA	9456	ARM	Social Sectors Reform Program (Supplementary)	0.55	4-Dec-2020	4-Dec-2020							
CWRD	TA	6570	GEO	Supporting High-Level Technology for Asset Management	0.23	30-Sep-2020	30-Sep-2020	✓	✓	✓	✓	✓	✓	✓
EARD	Grant	0684	MON	Community Vegetable Farming for Livelihood Improvement	0.50	12-Feb-2020	19-May-2020	✓	✓	✓			✓	✓
EARD	Grant	0696	MON	First Utility-Scale Energy Storage	3.00	22-Apr-2020	14-May-2020	✓	✓	✓			✓	
EARD	TA	9887	MON	Sustainable Fodder Management (Supplementary)	0.40	26-Aug-2020	26-Aug-2020	✓	✓	✓			✓	✓
PARD	TA	9984	NAU	Digital Twin Capabilities in Project Management	0.23	21-May-2020	21-May-2020	✓	✓					
PARD	TA	9601	REG	Developing the Health Sector in the Pacific (Supplementary)	0.50	24-Apr-2020	24-Apr-2020							
SDCC	TA	9928	REG	Developing Innovative Community-Based Long-Term Care Systems and Services (Supplementary)	0.60	11-Dec-2020	11-Dec-2020	✓	✓					
SDCC	TA	6672	REG	Empowering Developing Member Countries to Use Multispectral Satellite Images and Artificial Intelligence for Land Use and Coastal Planning	0.30	11-Dec-2020	11-Dec-2020	✓	✓	✓	✓	✓	✓	✓
SDCC	TA	9420	REG	Implementation of Sustainable Transport for All (Supplementary)	1.10	15-Aug-2020	15-Aug-2020							
SDCC	TA	9170	REG	Promoting Smart Systems in ADB's Future Cities Program (Supplementary)	0.50	17-Apr-2020	17-Apr-2020							
SDCC	TA	9950	REG	Regional Support to Address the Outbreak of Coronavirus Disease 2019 and Potential Outbreaks of Other Communicable Diseases (Supplementary)	0.30	16-Nov-2020	16-Nov-2020	✓	✓	✓			✓	✓

continued on next page

Fund Name/ RD	Product Type	Product Approval Number	DMC	Project Title	ADB Approved Amount	Approval Date	Signing Date	OP1	OP2	OP3	OP4	OP5	OP6	OP7
SDCC	TA	6563	REG	Regional Support to Build Disease Resilient and Energy Efficient Centralized Air-conditioning Systems	0.50	12-Sep-2020	12-Sep-2020	✓	✓	✓	✓	✓	✓	✓
SDCC	TA	9634	REG	Strengthening Integrated Flood Risk Management (Supplementary)	0.06	11-Jun-2020	11-Jun-2020							
SDCC	TA	9965	REG	Support for Innovation and Technology Partnerships in Asia and the Pacific–High-Level Technology Application to Address Development Challenges (Subproject 3)	3.00	1-Apr-2020	1-Apr-2020	✓		✓				
SERD	TA	9609	INO	Building Inclusive Social Assistance (Supplementary)	1.00	24-Jul-2020	24-Jul-2020							
SERD	TA	9678	INO	Supporting the Advanced Knowledge and Skills for Sustainable Growth Project (Supplementary)	0.50	13-Mar-2020	13-Mar-2020							
SERD	TA	9079	PHI	Strengthening Social Protection Reforms (Supplementary)	1.00	10-Jul-2020	10-Jul-2020							
Integrated Disaster Risk Management Fund														
OGC	TA	9159	REG	Legal Readiness for Climate Finance and Climate Investments (Supplementary)	0.10	6-Feb-2020	6-Feb-2020							
SDCC	TA	9728	REG	Scoping of Community Resilience Partnership Program (Supplementary)	0.15	24-Mar-2020	24-Mar-2020	✓	✓			✓		
Investment Climate Facilitation Fund														
ERCD	TA	6592	REG	Building Financial Resilience and Stability to Reinvigorate Growth	0.90	21-Nov-2020	21-Nov-2020		✓				✓	✓
ERCD	TA	9957	REG	Enhance AsianBondsOnline as the Primary Bond Information Platform in ASEAN+3	2.00	11-Mar-2020	11-Mar-2020			✓			✓	✓
ERCD	TA	6641	REG	Support for ASEAN+3 Bond Market Forum under the Asian Bond Markets Initiative Medium-Term Road Map, 2019–2022	1.80	7-Dec-2020	7-Dec-2020						✓	✓
Ireland Trust Fund for Building Climate Change and Disaster Resilience in Small Island Developing States														
PARD	TA	9464	REG	Pacific Disaster Resilience Program (Supplementary)	1.00	7-Sep-2020	7-Sep-2020							
PARD	TA	9963	REG	Strengthening Social Protection in the Pacific (Supplementary)	1.00	24-Jul-2020	24-Jul-2020	✓	✓	✓			✓	✓

continued on next page

Fund Name/ RD	Product Type	Product Approval Number	DMC	Project Title	ADB Approved Amount	Approval Date	Signing Date	OP1	OP2	OP3	OP4	OP5	OP6	OP7
SDCC	TA	9950	REG	Regional Support to Address the Outbreak of Coronavirus Disease 2019 and Potential Outbreaks of Other Communicable Diseases (Supplementary)	0.30	16-Jun-2020	16-Jun-2020	✓	✓	✓			✓	✓
Japan Fund for Information and Communication Technology														
CWRD	Grant	9207	TAJ	Skills and Employability Enhancement	1.50	30-Jun-2020	21-Oct-2020	✓	✓				✓	
Japan Fund for Poverty Reduction														
CWRD	TA	6635	KAZ	Institutional Support to the National Quality Center for Road Assets	1.00	4-Dec-2020	26-Dec-2020	✓	✓		✓		✓	
EARD	Grant	9204	MON	Improving Transport Services in *Ger* Areas	2.00	10-Dec-2019	19-May-2020	✓	✓		✓		✓	
EARD	Grant	9206	MON	Managing Solid Waste in Secondary Cities	2.00	8-Jun-2020	2-Jul-2020	✓	✓	✓	✓	✓	✓	✓
EARD	Grant	9208	MON	Support for Inclusive Education	2.00	3-Jul-2020	15-Sep-2020	✓	✓				✓	
EARD	Grant	9202	MON	Ulaanbaatar Community Food Waste Recycling	3.00	7-Oct-2019	17-Jan-2020	✓	✓	✓	✓		✓	✓
EARD	Grant	9205	MON	Vegetable Production and Irrigated Agriculture	2.00	27-Feb-2020	5-May-2020	✓	✓	✓		✓		
EARD	TA	9880	MON	Strengthening Capacity on Disaster Risk Assessment, Reduction, and Transfer Instruments in Mongolia	2.00	2-Dec-2019	17-Apr-2020	✓	✓	✓			✓	✓
EARD	TA	6534	MON	Strengthening Integrated Early Warning System in Mongolia	0.50	14-Jul-2020	30-Jul-2020	✓	✓	✓			✓	✓
ERCD	TA	6556	REG	Challenges and Opportunities of Population Aging in Asia: Improving Data and Analysis for Healthy and Productive Aging	2.00	2-Sep-2020	2-Sep-2020	✓	✓				✓	✓
ERCD	TA	6536	REG	Nowcasting and Disasters: Impact-Based Forecasting and Socioeconomic Monitoring	2.00	10-Jul-2020	10-Jul-2020		✓	✓			✓	
PARD	Grant	9212	PAL	Disaster Resilient Clean Energy Financing	3.00	27-Oct-2020	1-Dec-2020	✓	✓	✓			✓	
SARD	Grant	9211	BHU	Alternative Renewable Energy Pilot	3.00	21-Oct-2020	6-Nov-2020	✓	✓	✓		✓	✓	
SARD	Grant	9217	IND	Assam Power Sector Investment Program–Tranche 3	2.00	7-Dec-2020	30-Dec-2020	✓	✓	✓			✓	
SARD	Grant	9210	IND	Delhi-Meerut Regional Rapid Transit System Investment–Tranche 1	3.00	26-Aug-2020	8-Sep-2020	✓	✓	✓	✓		✓	

continued on next page

Fund Name/ RD	Product Type	Product Approval Number	DMC	Project Title	ADB Approved Amount	Approval Date	Signing Date	OP1	OP2	OP3	OP4	OP5	OP6	OP7
SARD	Grant	9213	IND	Meghalaya Power Distribution Sector Improvement	2.00	30-Oct-2020	1-Dec-2020	✓	✓	✓		✓	✓	
SARD	Grant	9214	SRI	Small and Medium-Sized Enterprises Line of Credit Project–Third Additional Financing	1.25	23-Nov-2020	25-Nov-2020	✓	✓	✓		✓	✓	
SARD	TA	9883	BAN	Support to Quality Enhancement in Primary Education	1.20	4-Dec-2019	3-Aug-2020	✓	✓				✓	
SARD	TA	6537	BHU	Improving Market Linkages for Cottage and Small Industries	2.00	9-Jul-2020	16-Jul-2020	✓	✓				✓	✓
SARD	TA	6636	IND	Enhancing Community Participation, Gender Mainstreaming, and Institutional Capacity Building of Uttar Pradesh Power Corporation Limited	1.50	4-Dec-2020	31-Dec-2020	✓	✓	✓		✓	✓	
SARD	TA	6658	IND	Strengthening Capacity for Comprehensive Primary Health Care in Urban Areas	2.00	8-Dec-2020	31-Dec-2020	✓	✓		✓		✓	
SARD	TA	6609	SRI	Value Chain Development for Tea Sector	1.75	23-Nov-2020	9-Dec-2020	✓	✓	✓		✓	✓	
SDCC	TA	9955	REG	Building Disaster-Resilient Infrastructure through Enhanced Knowledge	2.00	9-Mar-2020	9-Mar-2020	✓	✓	✓			✓	
SDCC	TA	6539	REG	Investing in Climate Change Adaptation through Agroecological Landscape Restoration: A Nature-Based Solution for Climate Resilience	2.00	14-Jul-2020	14-Jul-2020		✓	✓		✓		
SDCC	TA	6669	REG	Promoting Action on Plastic Pollution from Source to Sea in Asia and the Pacific–Prioritizing and Implementing Actions to Reduce Marine Plastic Pollution (Subproject 2)	1.50	11-Dec-2020	11-Dec-2020	✓	✓	✓		✓	✓	✓
SERD	Grant	9216	CAM	Agricultural Value Chain Competitiveness and Safety Enhancement	3.00	26-Nov-2020	7-Dec-2020	✓	✓	✓		✓		✓
SERD	Grant	9215	INO	Sustainable Energy Access in Eastern Indonesia–Electricity Grid Development Program (Phase 2)	3.00	24-Nov-2020	8-Dec-2020	✓	✓	✓		✓	✓	
SERD	Grant	9209	TIM	Coffee and Agroforestry Livelihood Improvement	3.00	28-May-2020	13-Jul-2020	✓	✓			✓	✓	
SERD	TA	9913	PHI	Strengthening the Transition of Vulnerable Communities Affected by the Malolos–Clark Railway Project	2.00	18-Dec-2019	20-May-2020	✓	✓				✓	

continued on next page

Fund Name/ RD	Product Type	Product Approval Number	DMC	Project Title	ADB Approved Amount	Approval Date	Signing Date	OP1	OP2	OP3	OP4	OP5	OP6	OP7
SERD	TA	9681	REG	Southeast Asia Agriculture, Natural Resources, and Rural Development Facility (Supplementary)	1.30	7-Sep-2020	7-Sep-2020							
SERD	TA	9554	REG	Southeast Asia Urban Services Facility (Supplementary)	4.00	9-Jun-2020	9-Jun-2020							
SERD	TA	6671	REG	Technology-Enabled Innovation in Education in Southeast Asia	2.00	11-Dec-2020	11-Dec-2020	✓	✓				✓	✓
SERD	TA	9993	THA	Climate Change Adaptation in Agriculture for Enhanced Recovery and Sustainability of Highlands	2.00	19-Jun-2020	11-Aug-2020	✓	✓	✓		✓	✓	✓
SDCC	TA	6612	REG	COVID-19 Infection Prevention and Control through an Integrated Water, Sanitation, Hygiene, and Health Approach	2.00	25-Nov-2020	25-Nov-2020	✓	✓	✓	✓	✓	✓	✓
SDCC	TA	6594	REG	Mitigating the Impact of COVID-19 through Community-Led Interventions	2.00	16-Nov-2020	16-Nov-2020	✓	✓				✓	✓
Japan Fund for the Joint Crediting Mechanism														
SARD	Grant	0733	MLD	Greater Male Waste-to-Energy	10.00	12-Aug-2020	28-Sep-2020	✓	✓	✓	✓		✓	
Leading Asia's Private Infrastructure Fund														
PSOD	Equity	JL09	IND	Avaada Solar Phase 2	7.50	22-Sep-2020	28-Sep-2020							
PSOD	Equity	7636	REG	Asian Sustainable Infrastructure Mobilization	45.00	8-Jul-2020	8-Sep-2020							
PSOD	Loan	8378	AFG	Afghan Power Plant Company Limited Mazar Gas-Fired Power	10.00	20-Feb-2020	15-Jun-2020							
PSOD	Loan	8381	BAN	Reliance Bangladesh Liquefied Natural Gas and Power–Additional Financing	100.00	18-Jun-2020	30-Jul-2020							
PSOD	Loan	8382	GEO	Georgian Green Bond	20.00	22-Jul-2020	23-Jul-2020							
PSOD	Loan	8386	REG	Indorama Ventures Regional Blue Loan	50.00	23-Nov-2020	24-Nov-2020							
PSOD	Loan	8379	VIE	B.Grimm Viet Nam Solar Power	9.30	8-Apr-2020	5-Jun-2020							
PSOD	Loan	8373	VIE	Gulf Solar Power	7.60	5-Nov-2019	28-Jan-2020							
People's Republic of China Poverty Reduction and Regional Cooperation Fund														
CWRD	TA	9839	PAK	Preparing Urban Development Projects (Supplementary)	1.50	21-May-2020	21-May-2020	✓	✓	✓	✓	✓	✓	✓
CWRD	TA	6535	REG	Addressing Health Threats in Central Asia Regional Economic Cooperation Countries and the Caucasus	0.40	13-Jul-2020	13-Jul-2020	✓	✓				✓	✓

continued on next page

Fund Name/ RD	Product Type	Product Approval Number	DMC	Project Title	ADB Approved Amount	Approval Date	Signing Date	OP1	OP2	OP3	OP4	OP5	OP6	OP7
CWRD	TA	6694	REG	Supporting the Central Asia Regional Economic Cooperation Institute	1.00	18-Dec-2020	18-Dec-2020		✓	✓			✓	✓
CWRD	TA	9987	UZB	Road Subsector Development Strategy and Action Plan (Supplementary)	0.50	21-Aug-2020	21-Aug-2020		✓	✓			✓	✓
EARD	TA	9938	MON	Methane Gas Supply Chain Development Master Plan	0.50	26-Dec-2019	25-Jan-2020	✓					✓	
EARD	TA	6699	REG	Enhancing Knowledge as Public Goods for Project Innovation, Demonstration, and Replication	0.50	23-Dec-2020	23-Dec-2020	✓	✓				✓	
EARD	TA	6558	REG	Strengthening Knowledge and Capacities for the Design and Implementation of Free Trade Agreements Involving Central Asia Regional Economic Cooperation Countries	0.50	31-Aug-2020	31-Aug-2020		✓				✓	✓
ERCD	TA	6592	REG	Building Financial Resilience and Stability to Reinvigorate Growth	0.15	21-Nov-2020	21-Nov-2020		✓				✓	✓
ERCD	TA	9953	REG	Creating Ecosystems for Green Local Currency Bonds for Infrastructure Development in ASEAN+3	0.50	4-Mar-2020	4-Mar-2020			✓			✓	✓
PARD	TA	9963	REG	Strengthening Social Protection in the Pacific	0.50	15-Apr-2020	15-Apr-2020	✓	✓	✓			✓	✓
SDCC	TA	9950	REG	Regional Support to Address the Outbreak of Coronavirus Disease 2019 and Potential Outbreaks of Other Communicable Diseases (Supplementary)	2.00	8-Apr-2020	8-Apr-2020	✓	✓	✓			✓	✓
SERD	TA	9916	REG	Greater Mekong Subregion Sustainable Agriculture and Food Security Program	0.75	25-Mar-2020	25-Mar-2020	✓	✓	✓		✓	✓	✓
SERD	TA	9971	REG	Southeast Asia Agriculture, Natural Resources, and Rural Development Facility–Phase II (Supplementary)	1.20	31-Aug-2020	31-Aug-2020	✓	✓	✓		✓	✓	✓
Regional Cooperation and Integration Fund														
CWRD	TA	6535	REG	Addressing Health Threats in Central Asia Regional Economic Cooperation Countries and the Caucasus	0.50	13-Jul-2020	13-Jul-2020	✓	✓				✓	✓
CWRD	TA	9630	REG	Assessing Economic Corridor Development Potential Among Kazakhstan, Uzbekistan, and Tajikistan (Supplementary)	1.00	18-Nov-2020	18-Nov-2020							

continued on next page

Fund Name/ RD	Product Type	Product Approval Number	DMC	Project Title	ADB Approved Amount	Approval Date	Signing Date	OP1	OP2	OP3	OP4	OP5	OP6	OP7
CWRD	TA	6591	REG	Enhancing Road Safety for Central Asia Regional Economic Cooperation Member Countries (Phase 2)	1.20	13-Nov-2020	13-Nov-2020	✓	✓				✓	✓
CWRD	TA	9709	REG	Regional Cooperation on Increasing Cross-Border Energy Trading within the Central Asian Power System–Modernization of Coordinating Dispatch Center Energiya (Subproject 1) (Supplementary)	0.45	19-Nov-2020	19-Nov-2020		✓	✓			✓	✓
CWRD	TA	6589	REG	Supporting Economic Corridor Development in Armenia and Georgia to Enhance Trade and Competitiveness	0.70	31-Oct-2020	31-Oct-2020		✓				✓	✓
EARD	TA	6660	PRC	Enhancing the Sustainable Cooperation of Yunnan and Guizhou with the Greater Mekong Subregion	0.45	8-Dec-2020	30-Dec-2020			✓				✓
EARD	TA	6687	PRC	Supporting Sustainable Finance and Regional Cooperation	0.80	17-Dec-2020	31-Dec-2020			✓			✓	✓
PARD	TA	9968	REG	Preparing Projects to Enhance Transport Connectivity and Resilience in the Pacific (Supplementary)	0.70	4-Dec-2020	4-Dec-2020	✓	✓	✓			✓	✓
SARD	TA	6528	REG	Strengthening the Implementation of Regional Cooperation and Integration Initiatives of South Asian Association for Regional Cooperation	0.50	29-Jun-2020	29-Jun-2020	✓	✓				✓	✓
SDCC	TA	6628	REG	Promoting Innovations in Regional Cooperation and Integration in the Aftermath of COVID-19	0.50	3-Dec-2020	3-Dec-2020	✓	✓	✓			✓	✓
SDCC	TA	6561	REG	Strengthening the Enabling Environment for Disaster Risk Financing (Phase 2)	0.50	9-Sep-2020	9-Sep-2020	✓	✓	✓			✓	✓
SERD	TA	9916	REG	Greater Mekong Subregion Sustainable Agriculture and Food Security Program (Second Supplementary)	1.00	20-Oct-2020	20-Oct-2020	✓	✓	✓		✓	✓	✓
SERD	TA	9971	REG	Southeast Asia Agriculture, Natural Resources, and Rural Development Facility–Phase II (Supplementary)	1.00	31-Aug-2020	31-Aug-2020	✓	✓	✓		✓	✓	✓
SERD	TA	6542	TIM	Capacity for Multilateral and Regional Economic Integration	0.50	22-Jul-2020	11-Aug-2020		✓					✓

continued on next page

Fund Name/ RD	Product Type	Product Approval Number	DMC	Project Title	ADB Approved Amount	Approval Date	Signing Date	OP1	OP2	OP3	OP4	OP5	OP6	OP7
Republic of Korea e-Asia and Knowledge Partnership Fund														
CWRD	TA	6650	AZE	Fostering Development of Local Tech Startups	0.50	3-Dec-2020	30-Dec-2020	✓	✓				✓	
CWRD	TA	9946	KAZ	Promoting Digital Technologies for Sustainable Development	0.50	9-Jan-2020	4-Feb-2020						✓	
CWRD	TA	6564	KAZ	Supporting Renewable Technology-Inclusive Heat Supply Legislation	0.50	14-Sep-2020	25-Sep-2020		✓	✓			✓	
CWRD	TA	6602	REG	Supporting Startup Ecosystem in the Central Asia Regional Economic Cooperation Region to Mitigate Impact of COVID-19 and Support Economic Revival	0.50	18-Nov-2020	18-Nov-2020		✓				✓	✓
CWRD	TA	9987	UZB	Road Subsector Development Strategy and Action Plan	0.50	2-Jun-2020	26-Jun-2020		✓	✓			✓	✓
EARD	TA	9906	MON	Improving Transport Services in *Ger* Areas	0.50	10-Dec-2019	9-Jan-2020	✓	✓			✓	✓	
EARD	TA	9938	MON	Methane Gas Supply Chain Development Master Plan	0.50	26-Dec-2019	25-Jan-2020	✓					✓	
ERCD	TA	6592	REG	Building Financial Resilience and Stability to Reinvigorate Growth	0.15	21-Nov-2020	21-Nov-2020		✓				✓	✓
ERCD	TA	6600	REG	Promoting Cross-Border Financial Transactions in the ASEAN+3 Region: Support to the Cross-Border Settlement Infrastructure Forum under the Asian Bond Markets Initiative Medium-Term Road Map, 2019–2022	0.50	18-Nov-2020	18-Nov-2020						✓	✓
ERCD	TA	6585	REG	Impact Evaluation of Financial Technology Innovations in Selected Developing Member Countries	0.50	30-Oct-2020	30-Oct-2020	✓	✓					
PARD	TA	9968	REG	Preparing Projects to Enhance Transport Connectivity and Resilience in the Pacific	0.50	4-Dec-2020	4-Dec-2020	✓	✓	✓			✓	✓
PARD	TA	9963	REG	Strengthening Social Protection in the Pacific	0.50	15-Apr-2020	15-Apr-2020	✓	✓	✓			✓	✓
SARD	TA	9980	IND	Strengthening Universal Health Coverage in India: Supporting the Implementation of Pradhan Mantri Jan Arogya Yojana	0.50	14-May-2020	22-Jun-2020	✓	✓				✓	
SARD	TA	6529	REG	Planning for Economic Recovery of South Asia from COVID-19	0.50	26-Nov-2020	26-Nov-2020	✓	✓			✓	✓	✓

continued on next page

Fund Name/ RD	Product Type	Product Approval Number	DMC	Project Title	ADB Approved Amount	Approval Date	Signing Date	OP1	OP2	OP3	OP4	OP5	OP6	OP7
SDCC	TA	6672	REG	Empowering Developing Member Countries to Use Multispectral Satellite Images and Artificial Intelligence for Land Use and Coastal Planning	0.50	11-Dec-2020	11-Dec-2020	✓	✓	✓	✓	✓	✓	✓
SDCC	TA	9943	REG	Facilitating Knowledge for Innovation and Technology Cooperation to Accelerate Development	0.75	31-Jan-2020	31-Jan-2020						✓	
SDCC	TA	9960	REG	Integrated High Impact Innovation in Sustainable Energy Technology: Pilot Testing of Innovative Energy Technologies and Business Models (Subproject 3)	0.15	1-Apr-2020	1-Apr-2020	✓	✓	✓	✓	✓	✓	✓
SDCC	TA	6669	REG	Promoting Action on Plastic Pollution from Source to Sea in Asia and the Pacific-Prioritizing and Implementing Actions to Reduce Marine Plastic Pollution (Subproject 2)	0.50	11-Dec-2020	11-Dec-2020	✓	✓	✓	✓	✓	✓	✓
SDCC	TA	9461	REG	Protecting and Investing in Natural Capital in Asia and the Pacific (Supplementary)	0.50	28-Feb-2020	28-Feb-2020							
SDCC	TA	9950	REG	Regional Support to Address the Outbreak of Coronavirus Disease 2019 and Potential Outbreaks of Other Communicable Diseases (Supplementary)	2.00	8-Apr-2020	8-Apr-2020	✓	✓	✓			✓	✓
SDCC	TA	6645	REG	Strengthening Resilience and Stability of Banking and Nonbank Financial Systems in Asia	0.75	7-Dec-2020	7-Dec-2020	✓	✓				✓	✓
SDCC	TA	9967	REG	Using Digital Technology to Improve National Health Insurance in Asia and the Pacific	1.00	24-Apr-2020	24-Apr-2020	✓	✓				✓	
SERD	TA	6583	INO	Electric Transportation and Charging Infrastructure	0.20	27-Oct-2020	27-Oct-2020						✓	
SERD	TA	9572	REG	Enhancing Effectiveness of Subregional Programs to Advance Regional Cooperation and Integration in Southeast Asia (Supplementary)	0.50	9-Jul-2020	9-Jul-2020							
SERD	TA	9621	REG	Green and Innovative Finance Initiative for Scaling Up Southeast Asian Infrastructure (Supplementary)	1.50	10-Jul-2020	10-Jul-2020							

continued on next page

Fund Name/ RD	Product Type	Product Approval Number	DMC	Project Title	ADB Approved Amount	Approval Date	Signing Date	OP1	OP2	OP3	OP4	OP5	OP6	OP7
Sanitation Financing Partnership Trust Fund														
EARD	TA	9753	PRC	Preparing Environmental and Rural Development Projects (Supplementary)	0.45	13-Mar-2020	13-Mar-2020	✓	✓	✓		✓	✓	✓
EARD	TA	9753	PRC	Preparing Environmental and Rural Development Projects (Supplementary)	0.15	1-Jul-2020	1-Jul-2020	✓	✓	✓		✓	✓	✓
EARD	TA	9732	PRC	Preparing Urban and Social Development Projects (Supplementary)	0.10	14-Jan-2020	14-Jan-2020	✓	✓	✓	✓	✓	✓	✓
Strategic Climate Fund														
PARD	Grant	0764	KIR	South Tarawa Renewable Energy	3.70	26-Nov-2020	21-Dec-2020	✓	✓	✓			✓	
PSOD	TA	9959	IND	Gender Capacity Enhancement in Poultry (Supplementary)	0.20	20-Nov-2020	20-Nov-2020	✓	✓			✓		
SDCC	TA	6629	REG	Improved Decision-making for Climate-Resilient Development in Asia and the Pacific	2.15	1-Dec-2020	1-Dec-2020		✓	✓			✓	
SERD	Grant	0736	CAM	Grid Reinforcement	4.70	10-Sep-2020	12-Oct-2020	✓	✓	✓			✓	
United Kingdom Fund for Asia Regional Trade and Connectivity														
CWRD	TA	9487	REG	Almaty–Bishkek Economic Corridor Support (Supplementary)	0.75	29-Apr-2020	29-Apr-2020							
CWRD	TA	6540	REG	Fostering Expanded Regional Electricity and Gas Interconnection and Trade under the CAREC Energy Strategy 2030	2.50	15-Jul-2020	15-Jul-2020	✓	✓				✓	✓
EARD	TA	6558	REG	Strengthening Knowledge and Capacities for the Design and Implementation of Free Trade Agreements Involving Central Asia Regional Economic Cooperation Countries	0.70	31-Aug-2020	31-Aug-2020		✓				✓	✓
SDCC	TA	9420	REG	Implementation of Sustainable Transport for All (Supplementary)	1.20	9-Dec-2020	9-Dec-2020							
SDCC	TA	6628	REG	Promoting Innovations in Regional Cooperation and Integration in the Aftermath of COVID-19	2.00	3-Dec-2020	3-Dec-2020	✓	✓	✓			✓	✓
SERD	TA	6579	REG	"Early Harvest" Implementation of the Cross-Border Transport and Trade Facilitation in the Greater Mekong Subregion	1.50	22-Oct-2020	22-Oct-2020							✓

continued on next page

Fund Name/ RD	Product Type	Product Approval Number	DMC	Project Title	ADB Approved Amount	Approval Date	Signing Date	OP1	OP2	OP3	OP4	OP5	OP6	OP7
Urban Climate Change Resilience Trust Fund														
SARD	TA	9829	IND	Strengthening Climate Change Resilience in Urban India–Strengthening Smart Urban Mass Rapid Transit and Climate Change Resilience in the National Capital Region (Subproject 3)	2.89	22-Oct-2019	26-Jun-2020	✓	✓	✓			✓	
SDCC	TA	9960	REG	Integrated High Impact Innovation in Sustainable Energy Technology: Pilot Testing of Innovative Energy Technologies and Business Models (Subproject 3)	0.45	1-Apr-2020	1-Apr-2020	✓	✓	✓	✓	✓	✓	✓
SDCC	TA	9660	REG	Promoting Transformative Gender Equality Agenda in Asia and the Pacific (Supplementary)	0.74	9-Jul-2020	9-Jul-2020	✓	✓	✓	✓		✓	
Water Financing Partnership Facility (Multi-Donor Trust Fund)														
SERD	TA	9971	REG	Southeast Asia Agriculture, Natural Resources, and Rural Development Facility–Phase II	0.15	29-Apr-2020	29-Apr-2020	✓	✓	✓		✓	✓	✓
Water Financing Partnership Facility (Netherlands)														
CWRD	TA	9442	PAK	Khyber Pakhtunkhwa Water Resources Development	0.30	20-Oct-2020	20-Oct-2020							
CWRD	TA	6663	PAK	Strengthening Food Security Post-COVID-19 and Locust Attacks	0.20	9-Dec-2020	9-Dec-2020	✓	✓	✓		✓	✓	
SARD	TA	9927	BAN	Preparing the Climate and Disaster Resilient Small-Scale Water Resources Management Project	0.75	24-Dec-2019	25-Mar-2020	✓	✓	✓		✓	✓	
SARD	TA	6546	BAN	Preparing the Climate-Resilient Livelihood Improvement and Watershed Management in Chittagong Hill Tracts Sector Project	0.50	6-Aug-2020	17-Dec-2020	✓	✓	✓		✓	✓	
SARD	TA	6568	NEP	Implementation Support for the Priority River Basin Flood Risk Management Project	0.75	28-Sep-2020	23-Oct-2020	✓	✓	✓		✓	✓	
SARD	TA	9443	REG	Strengthening Capacity to Design and Implement Water and Rural Infrastructure (Supplementary)	0.50	28-Sep-2020	28-Sep-2020							
SERD	TA	9323	LAO	Sustainable Rural Infrastructure and Watershed Management Sector (Supplementary)	0.50	10-Sep-2020	10-Sep-2020							

continued on next page

Fund Name/ RD	Product Type	Product Approval Number	DMC	Project Title	ADB Approved Amount	Approval Date	Signing Date	OP1	OP2	OP3	OP4	OP5	OP6	OP7
Women Entrepreneurs Finance Initiative														
PSOD	TA	6705	REG	Technical Assistance for the Women's Financing Marketplace–Subproject 3: Capacity Building	0.10	28-Dec-2020	28-Dec-2020	✓	✓					
PSOD	TA	6646	REG	Technical Assistance for the Women's Financing Marketplace–Subproject 2: Innovation and Technology	0.40	7-Dec-2020	7-Dec-2020	✓	✓					
SERD	Grant	0781	VIE	COVID-19 Relief for Women-Led Small and Medium-Sized Enterprises	5.00	9-Dec-2020	22-Dec-2020	✓	✓				✓	

ADB = Asian Development Bank, AFG = Afghanistan, ARM = Armenia, ASEAN = Association of Southeast Asian Nations, AZE = Azerbaijan, BAN = Bangladesh, BHU = Bhutan, CAM = Cambodia, CAREC = Central Asia Regional Economic Cooperation (Program), COO = Cook Islands, COVID-19 = coronavirus disease, CWRD = Central and West Asia Department, DMC= developing member country, EARD = East Asia Department, ERCD = Economic Research and Regional Cooperation Department, FIJ = Fiji, FSM = Federated States of Micronesia, GEO = Georgia, IND = India, INO = Indonesia, KAZ = Kazakhstan, KIR = Kiribati, LAO = Lao People's Democratic Republic, MLD = Maldives, MON = Mongolia, NAU = Nauru, NEP = Nepal, NIU = Niue, OGC = Office of the General Counsel, OP = operational priority, PAK = Pakistan, PAL = Palau, PARD = Pacific Department, PHI = Philippines, PNG = Papua New Guinea, PRC = People's Republic of China, PSOD = Private Sector Operations Department, RD = regional department, REG = regional, RMI = Marshall Islands, SAM = Samoa, SARD = South Asia Department, SDCC = Sustainable Development and Climate Change Department, SERD = Southeast Asia Department, SOL = Solomon Islands, SRI = Sri Lanka, TA = technical assistance, TAJ = Tajikistan, THA = Thailand, TIM = Timor–Leste, TON = Tonga, TUV = Tuvalu, UZB = Uzbekistan, VAN = Vanuatu, VIE = Viet Nam.

Note: Classification started from April 2019 ADB-approved projects except (i) supplementary approvals for additional financing, and (ii) PSOD loans and equities. Strategy, Policy and Partnerships Department is reviewing the project's classification and may be subject to future adjustments.

Source: eOperations.

List of ADB Trust Funds, Global Funds, and Special Funds ($ million)

Fund Name	Cumulative Contribution Committed	Cumulative Approved Projects and Direct Charges	Cumulative Committed Projects and Direct Charges	Cumulative Disbursements
Trust Funds under Financing Partnership Facilities				
Clean Energy Financing Partnership Facility				
1 Asian Clean Energy Fund	55.7	54.4	49.4	40.9
2 Canadian Climate Fund for the Private Sector in Asia	80.1	50.9	50.9	52.3
3 Carbon Capture and Storage Fund	58.8	18.8	18.8	12.9
4 Clean Energy Fund	131.8	89.6	87.6	61.3
Health Financing Partnership Facility				
5 Regional Malaria and Other Communicable Disease Threats Trust Fund	36.0	26.8	26.8	28.2
Regional Cooperation and Integration Financing Partnership Facility				
6 Regional Cooperation and Integration Fund[a]	99.6	77.8	77.8	62.9
7 Investment Climate Facilitation Fund	31.5	28.6	28.6	21.6
8 United Kingdom Fund for Asia Regional Trade and Connectivity	28.9	20.4	20.4	4.7
Urban Financing Partnership Facility				
9 ASEAN Australia Smart Cities Trust Fund	14.6	10.3	10.3	0.7
10 Cities Development Initiative for Asia Trust Fund	9.2	7.6	7.6	1.8
11 Urban Environmental Infrastructure Fund	21.5	20.2	20.2	16.9
12 Urban Climate Change Resilience Trust Fund	144.5	108.4	108.4	41.7
Water Financing Partnership Facility				
13 Netherlands Trust Fund	44.2	40.2	40.2	33.9
14 Multi-Donor Trust Fund	52.4	50.5	50.5	50.2
15 Sanitation Financing Partnership Trust Fund	19.0	17.3	17.3	11.8
ADB Ventures Financing Partnership Facility				
16 ADB Ventures Investment Fund 1[b]	59.7	–	–	–
ADB Ventures Investment Fund 2[b]	4.0	–	–	–

continued on next page

Fund Name	Cumulative Contribution Committed	Cumulative Approved Projects and Direct Charges	Cumulative Committed Projects and Direct Charges	Cumulative Disbursements
Stand-alone Trust Funds				
17 Afghanistan Infrastructure Trust Fund	773.2	570.4	570.4	338.5
18 Asia Pacific Climate Finance Fund	33.8	4.5	4.5	0.3
19 Asia Pacific Project Preparation Facility[c]	63.3	63.3	63.3	15.0
Australian Technical Assistance Grant	61.7	56.4	56.4	59.4
Canadian Cooperation Fund on Climate Change	3.4	3.7	3.7	3.8
20 Canadian Climate Fund for the Private Sector in Asia II[b]	149.5	–	–	–
21 Cooperation Fund for Project Preparation in the Greater Mekong Subregion and in Other Specific Asian Countries	8.5	6.2	6.2	5.2
22 Cooperation Fund for Regional Trade and Financial Security Initiative	2.8	2.6	2.6	2.7
Danish Cooperation Fund for Renewable Energy and Energy Efficiency in Rural Areas	3.6	3.5	3.5	3.6
23 Domestic Resource Mobilization Trust Fund	7.2	3.5	3.5	2.1
Financial Sector Development Partnership Fund	6.4	5.9	5.9	6.1
24 Future Carbon Fund	115.0	53.0	57.4	50.6
Gender and Development Cooperation Fund	11.7	11.9	11.9	12.4
Governance Cooperation Fund	7.2	7.2	7.2	7.6
25 High-Level Technology Fund	70.3	39.6	39.6	4.0
26 Integrated Disaster Risk Management Fund	9.7	8.0	8.0	8.1
27 Ireland Trust Fund for Building Climate Change and Disaster Resilience in Small Island Developing States	14.4	2.4	2.4	0.3
28 Japan Fund for Information and Communication Technology	10.7	11.1	9.6	9.2
29 Japan Fund for Poverty Reduction	930.6	856.4	830.9	725.0
Japan Fund for Public Policy Training	22.0	13.7	13.7	16.1
30 Japan Fund for the Joint Crediting Mechanism	80.4	42.7	42.7	11.7
31 Japan Scholarship Program	191.6	189.2	189.2	192.1
32 Leading Asia's Private Sector Infrastructure Fund[d]	1,500.0	–	–	–
33 People's Republic of China Poverty Reduction and Regional Cooperation Fund	90.0	59.4	59.4	45.6
34 Project Readiness Improvement Trust Fund	7.8	7.3	7.3	5.7

continued on next page

Fund Name	Cumulative Contribution Committed	Cumulative Approved Projects and Direct Charges	Cumulative Committed Projects and Direct Charges	Cumulative Disbursements
35 Republic of Korea e-Asia and Knowledge Partnership Fund	122.2	73.4	72.4	58.5
Second Danish Cooperation Fund for Renewable Energy and Energy Efficiency in Rural Areas	3.5	3.5	3.5	3.7
36 Spanish Cooperation Fund for Technical Assistance	14.4	10.2	10.2	11.2
37 Australian Climate Finance Partnership	106.0	–	–	–
Global Funds				
38a and b Climate Investment Funds	1,448.1	1,049.4	1,040.6	693.3
39 Global Agriculture and Food Security Program	67.5	61.8	61.8	36.8
40 Global Environment Facility	245.8	180.5	180.5	185.6
41 Global Partnership for Education	1.4	1.8	1.8	1.1
42 Green Climate Fund	374.7	472.5	472.5	41.4
43 Women Entrepreneurs Finance Initiative	31.1	23.2	18.2	7.8
Special Funds				
44 Asia Pacific Disaster Response Fund[e]	165.0	122.4	118.4	113.3
45 Climate Change Fund	98.0	75.1	75.1	57.3
46 Financial Sector Development Partnership Special Fund	23.0	20.0	19.6	10.7
Japan Special Fund (includes ACCSF)	1,065.2	1,075.2	1,075.2	1,075.3
Total	**8,831.8**	**6,641.6**	**6,570.2**	**4,773.1**

ADB = Asian Development Bank, ASEAN = Association of Southeast Asian Nations, ACCSF = Asian Currency Crisis Support Facility.
Figures may not add up due to rounding.
[a] Special Fund.
[b] Project approvals, commitments, and disbursements of trust funds for nonsovereign operations are commercially sensitive information and cannot be disclosed to the public.
[c] Out of the $63.3 million approved technical assistance and direct charges, $50.6 million have been allocated by the Steering Committee.
[d] Cumulative contribution committed refers to total amount pledged of $1.5 billion. These contributions are formally recognized and recorded in ADB's system and financial statements once they are remitted by the financing partner to ADB.
[e] Disbursement figure includes advances not yet liquidated.
Notes:
1. Excludes Credit Guarantee Investment Facility.
2. Cumulative contribution committed includes revaluation and devaluation of contributions not yet remitted to ADB; excludes investment income and foreign exchange gain (loss), hence, cumulative project and direct charges approval amount can be higher compared to cumulative contribution committed. For Green Climate Fund (GCF), ADB approval is requisite to GCF commitment.
3. Approved amount refers to the financing approved by ADB's Board of Directors or Management which may be in US dollars, special drawing rights or other currencies as applicable. Committed amount refers to financing for which a legal agreement has been signed by the borrower, recipient, or investee company and ADB. A commitment is recorded in ADB's accounts as of the date of the signing of the legal agreement.
4. Cumulative disbursements include project and direct charge expenditures and administrative expenses.
5. Cumulative Approved Projects and Direct Charges and Cumulative Committed Projects and Direct Charges are less of savings from financially completed projects and direct charges and cancellations.
6. The number on the first column is used as reference number for the Individual Fund Profiles in Appendix 5.
Sources: Cofinance Management System and December 2020 Status of Grants and Statement of Expenditures.

Individual Fund Profile

NOTES:

1. There are no fund profiles for the following:

   A. *Inactive funds waiting for completion of active projects.*
   1. Australian Technical Assistance Grant
   2. Canadian Cooperation Fund on Climate Change
   3. Danish Cooperation Fund for Renewable Energy and Energy Efficiency in Rural Areas
   4. Financial Sector Development Partnership Fund
   5. Gender and Development Cooperation Fund
   6. Governance Cooperation Fund
   7. Japan Fund for Public Policy Training
   8. Second Danish Cooperation Fund for Renewable Energy and Energy Efficiency in Rural Areas

   B. *Japan Special Fund*

2. Fund profile of Financial Sector Development Partnership Special Fund is included in the special fund.

3. The content of the individual fund profiles are based on Fund Manager teams' inputs.

4. Cumulative contribution committed are consistent with the *2020 ADB Annual Report* figures and includes revaluation and devaluation of contributions not yet remitted to ADB. It excludes investment income and foreign exchange gain (loss), hence, cumulative project and direct charges approved amount can be higher compared to cumulative contribution committed.

5. Net Available Balance figures are based on Fund Manager teams' inputs and are consistent with the *2020 ADB Annual Report*. Revisions and updated after cut-off were not considered.

1 ASIAN CLEAN ENERGY FUND
under the CLEAN ENERGY FINANCING PARTNERSHIP FACILITY (CEFPF–ACEF)

Donor: Japan

Year Established	2008
Financing Products	Grant Component of Investment (GCI), Technical Assistance (TA)
Objective	Support the efforts of developing member countries (DMCs) toward reducing greenhouse gases through utilization of renewable energy and energy efficiency technologies.
Eligible Sectors	Energy, Transport, Urban, and Agriculture
Facility Manager Alternate Facility Manager	Robert Guild, Chief Sector Officer, SDSC Kee-Yung Nam, Principal Energy Economist, SDSC-ENE

Financial Position as of 31 December 2020
(Amount in $ million)

Cumulative Donor Commitment	Net Balance Available for Trust Fund Committee Allocation		Number of Projects Funded (Approvals)	Number of Projects Funded (Commitments)
Amount	Amount	% of Commitment		
55.70	0.50	1%	43	42

Featured Project

TA 6680-REG: Preparing the Floating Solar Plus Program under the Pacific Renewable Energy Investment Facility	
Committed Amount	$2,000,000
Commitment Date	15 December 2020
Expected Completion Date	31 December 2024
Expected Outcome and/or Purpose	The transaction technical assistance facility aims to improve energy security in the Pacific. It will assess the potential for, and develop a road map of, financing floating photovoltaic projects in the 11 smallest Pacific island member countries.
Expected Results	The TA will conduct feasibility studies and due diligence to prepare floating solar PV projects in Kiribati, Tonga, and Tuvalu for approval within 2022–2023, as well as prefeasibility studies for the next three floating solar PV projects under the road map for potential ADB and private sector financing. With the implementation of these projects, Pacific island countries may rely less on imported fossil fuels for their energy needs and have sustainable, resilient, and low-carbon development in the region.

2020 Committed Projects

ADB Approved Number	Project Name
Grant 0753-INO	Sustainable Energy Access in Eastern Indonesia—Electricity Grid Development Program (Phase 2)
TA 9941-MON	Supporting Renewable Energy Development
TA 6680-REG	Preparing the Floating Solar Plus Program under the Pacific Renewable Energy Investment Facility

INO = Indonesia, MON = Mongolia, PV = photovoltaic, REG = regional, SDSC = Office of the Cluster Head of the Sustainable Development and Climate Change Department, SDSC-ENE = Energy Sector Group of the Sustainable Development and Climate Change Department.

2 CANADIAN CLIMATE FUND FOR THE PRIVATE SECTOR IN ASIA under the CLEAN ENERGY FINANCING PARTNERSHIP FACILITY (CFPS)

Donor: Canada

Year Established	2013
Financing Products	Loan, Technical Assistance (TA)
Objective	Catalyze private sector investment in climate change mitigation and adaptation.
Eligible Sectors	Energy, Transport, Urban, and Agriculture
Facility Manager Alternate Facility Manager	Robert Guild, Chief Sector Officer, SDSC Kee-Yung Nam, Principal Energy Economist, SDSC-ENE

Financial Position as of 31 December 2020
(Amount in $ million)

Cumulative Donor Commitment	Net Balance Available for Trust Fund Committee Allocation		Number of Projects Funded (Approvals)	Number of Projects Funded (Commitments)
Amount	Amount	% of Commitment		
80.08	2.7	3%	20	20

Featured Project

TA 9949-AFG: Herat Power Project	
Committed Amount	$225,000
Commitment Date	12 February 2020
Expected Completion Date	31 December 2021
Expected Outcome and/or Purpose	To spur economic growth in Afghanistan, the government with assistance from international donors, is focusing on expanding the availability of energy resources throughout the country. The TA will support the project development of the Herat Wind Power Project which will be the country's first grid-connected wind power project.
Expected Results	The ensuing project will (i) install about 25 MW new renewable energy capacity; (ii) generate about 111,143 MWh per year of electricity; (iii) reduce yearly emission by 33,343 tons of CO_2; and (iv) create employment, including those for women, during the operation of the project.

2020 Committed Projects

ADB Approved Number	Project Name
TA 9949-AFG	Herat Wind

AFG = Afghanistan, CO_2 = carbon dioxide, MW = megawatt, MWh = megawatt hour, SDSC = Office of the Cluster Head of the Sustainable Development and Climate Change Department, SDSC-ENE = Energy Sector Group of the Sustainable Development and Climate Change Department.

3 CARBON CAPTURE AND STORAGE FUND under the CLEAN ENERGY FINANCING PARTNERSHIP FACILITY (CEFPF–CCSF)

Donor: Global Carbon Capture and Storage Institute, the United Kingdom

Year Established	2009
Financing Products	Grant Component of Investment, Technical Assistance (TA), Direct Charge
Objective	Accelerate deployment of carbon capture and storage demonstration by promoting projects, engaging in capacity development, supporting geological investigations and environmental studies related to potential carbon dioxide storage sites, and undertaking community awareness and support programs.
Eligible Sectors	Energy and Transport
Facility Manager Alternate Facility Manager	Robert Guild, Chief Sector Officer, SDSC Kee-Yung Nam, Principal Energy Economist, SDSC-ENE

Financial Position as of 31 December 2020
(Amount in $ million)

Cumulative Donor Commitment	Net Balance Available for Trust Fund Committee Allocation		Number of Projects Funded (Approvals)	Number of Projects Funded (Commitments)
Amount	Amount	% of Commitment		
58.80	12.2	21%	13	13

Featured Project

TA 9686-REG: Integrated High Impact Innovation in Sustainable Energy Technology—Prefeasibility Analysis for Carbon Capture, Utilization, and Storage (Subproject 2)	
Committed Amount	$2,000,000
Commitment Date	13 December 2018
Expected Completion Date	30 September 2023
Expected Outcome and/or Purpose	The TA subproject 2 aims to increase the use of sustainable carbon capture, utilization and storage technologies in participating developing member countries.
Expected Results	TA subproject will focus on carbon utilization opportunities rather than storage-only approaches. The TA subproject will conduct feasibility analysis to determine the needs for additional support and potential demonstration and deployment. Input in feasibility studies will be sought from both the international, regional, and country experts and stakeholder communities. Studies will focus on costs, environmental and public health benefits, carbon footprint, sustainability and deployment considerations, technology development, and scalability for future investment.

REG = regional, SDSC = Office of the Cluster Head of the Sustainable Development and Climate Change Department, SDSC-ENE = Energy Sector Group of the Sustainable Development and Climate Change Department.

4 CLEAN ENERGY FUND
under the CLEAN ENERGY FINANCING PARTNERSHIP FACILITY (CEFPF–CEF)

Donors: Australia, Norway, Spain, Sweden, and the United Kingdom

Year Established	2007
Financing Products	Grant Component of Investment, Technical Assistance (TA), Direct Charge
Objective	Improve energy security in developing member countries and decrease the rate of climate change through increased use of clean energy.
Eligible Sectors	Energy, Transport, Urban, and Agriculture
Facility Manager Alternate Facility Manager	Robert Guild, Chief Sector Officer, SDSC Kee-Yung Nam, Principal Energy Economist, SDSC-ENE

Financial Position as of 31 December 2020
(Amount in $ million)

Cumulative Donor Commitment	Net Balance Available for Trust Fund Committee Allocation		Number of Projects Funded (Approvals)	Number of Projects Funded (Commitments)
Amount	Amount	% of Commitment		
131.80	27.54	21%	78	78

Featured Project

TA 6637-UZB: Promoting Distributed Solar Photovoltaic Systems for Enhanced Access to Energy	
Committed Amount	$1,000,000
Commitment Date	29 December 2020
Expected Completion Date	30 September 2022
Expected Outcome and/or Purpose	Uzbekistan's vast renewable energy resources are largely underdeveloped. The knowledge and support TA will promote the development of distributed solar photovoltaic (PV) systems in the country. Expansion of distributed solar PV systems will enhance energy access and fulfill the government's commitment to mitigate climate change impacts.
Expected Results	The TA will (i) support the development of the government's sector strategy for distributed solar systems to improve the quality of electricity supply in remote regions and to scale-up distributed solar systems through private investments; (ii) install at least 20-kilowatt distributed solar PV system to demonstrate the technical feasibility and socioeconomic benefits; and (iii) strengthen institutional capacity through hands on training in planning, designing, implementing, and operating the distributed solar PV systems.

2020 Committed Projects

ADB Approved Number	Project Name
Grant 0737-CAM	Grid Reinforcement Project
TA 6564-KAZ	Supporting Renewable Technology-Inclusive Heat Supply Legislation
TA 6560-PRC	Climate Change Financing Acceleration Platform
TA 6563-REG	Regional Support to Build Virus Resilient and Energy Efficient Centralized Air-conditioning Systems
TA 6619-REG	Marine Aquaculture, Reefs, Renewable Energy, and Ecotourism for Ecosystem Services
TA 9600-REG	Southeast Asia Energy Sector Development, Investment Planning, and Capacity Building Facility (Supplementary)
TA 9960-REG	Integrated High Impact Innovation in Sustainable Energy Technology: Pilot Testing of Innovative Energy Technologies and Business Models (Subproject 3)
TA 9389-SRI	Rooftop Solar Power Generation (Supplementary)
TA 6637-UZB	Promoting Distributed Solar Photovoltaic Systems for Enhanced Access to Energy

CAM = Cambodia, KAZ = Kazakhstan, PRC = People's Republic of China, REG = regional, SDSC = Office of the Cluster Head of the Sustainable Development and Climate Change Department, SDSC-ENE = Energy Sector Group of the Sustainable Development and Climate Change Department, SRI = Sri Lanka, UZB = Uzbekistan.

5 REGIONAL MALARIA AND OTHER COMMUNICABLE DISEASE THREATS TRUST FUND under the HEALTH FINANCING PARTNERSHIP FACILITY (HFPF–RMTF)

Donors: Australia, Canada, and the United Kingdom

Year Established	2013
Financing Products	Technical Assistance (TA), Grant, Direct Charge (DC)
Objective	To support developing member countries to develop multi-country, cross-border, and multisector responses to urgent malaria and other communicable disease issues.
Eligible Sectors	All developing member countries with focus on Greater Mekong Subregion countries
Facility Manager	Robert Guild, Chief Sector Officer, SDSC

Financial Position as of 31 December 2020
(Amount in $ million)

Cumulative Donor Commitment	Net Balance Available for Trust Fund Committee Allocation		Number of Projects Funded (Approvals)	Number of Projects Funded (Commitments)
Amount	Amount	% of Commitment		
36.00	0.7	2%	8	8

Featured Projects

TA 8959 REG: Malaria and Communicable Diseases Control in the Greater Mekong Subregion	
Committed Amount	$4,500,000
Commitment Date	23 September 2015
Completion Date	19 December 2018
Outcome and/or Purpose	National malaria and communicable diseases control (CDC) programs strengthened and better coordinated in Cambodia, the Lao People's Democratic Republic, and Myanmar
Results	(i) Myanmar malaria surveillance and diagnostic systems improved (ii) Migrant and mobile populations' specific needs for malaria prevention and treatment addressed (iii) Regional coordination on malaria and CDC among GMS countries strengthened

Grant 0448-0450 CAM, LAO, MYA: Second GMS Regional Communicable Diseases Control Project	
Committed Amount	$9,021,505.74
Commitment Date	4 January 2016
Completion Date	29 August 2018
Outcome and/or Purpose	Timely and adequate control of communicable diseases of regional relevance
Results	(i) Enhanced regional CDC systems (ii) Improved CDC along borders and economic corridors (iii) Integrated project management

2020 Committed Projects

Project Name
DC24: Contract extension for consultant Michael Peters (153064: RMTF Alignment to 2030) amounting to $20,000. The extension provided additional scope of work for COVID-19 initiatives.

CAM = Cambodia, COVID-19 = coronavirus disease, GMS = Greater Mekong Subregion, LAO = Lao People's Democratic Republic, MYA = Myanmar, REG = regional, SDSC = Office of the Cluster Head of the Sustainable Development and Climate Change Department.

6 REGIONAL COOPERATION AND INTEGRATION FUND under the REGIONAL COOPERATION AND INTEGRATION FINANCING PARTNERSHIP FACILITY (RCIFPF–RCIF)

Donors: ADB, Japan

Year Established	2007
Financing Products	Technical Assistance (TA)
Objective	The Regional Cooperation and Integration Fund (RCIF) is a special fund under the Regional Cooperation and Integration Financing Partnership Facility (RCIFPF) which aims to promote regional cooperation and integration (RCI) in Asia and the Pacific by financing TA projects that support greater and higher quality connectivity between economies, expand global and regional trade and investment opportunities, and increase and diversify regional public goods. The RCIF will prioritize TA projects that support one or more of the following innovations in RCI operations: (i) promoting sector and subsector diversification, (ii) expanding intersubregional cooperation, (iii) supporting development of new cross-border markets and geographic areas lagging in RCI, and (iv) increasing private sector participation in RCI. To encourage activities that are primarily regional in nature, priority is given to multi-country TA projects or projects supporting developing member countries (DMCs) as a group. Other factors for prioritization include (i) generation of RCI pipeline opportunities; (ii) application of multisector and/or cross-thematic approaches; (iii) enhancement of DMCs' resilience to pandemics such as the coronavirus disease; and (iv) support to vulnerable groups and segments of the economy in DMCs (such as small and medium-sized enterprises and women).
Eligible Sectors	All sectors are eligible for support from the RCIF
Facility Manager	Ronald Antonio Q. Butiong, Chief of Regional Cooperation and Integration Thematic Group, SDTC-RCI
Alternate Facility Manager	Yuebin Zhang, Principal Regional Cooperation Specialist, SDTC-RCI

Financial Position as of 31 December 2020
(Amount in $ million)

Cumulative Donor Commitment	Net Balance Available for Trust Fund Committee Allocation		Number of Projects Funded (Approvals)	Number of Projects Funded (Commitments)
Amount	Amount	% of Commitment		
99.63	25.2	25%	103	NA

Featured Project

TA 9487-REG: Almaty–Bishkek Economic Corridor Support	
Committed Amount	$2.50 million, of which $0.75 million is financed by RCIF
Commitment Date	15 December 2017
Expected Completion Date	31 December 2021

TA 9487-REG: Almaty–Bishkek Economic Corridor Support

Expected Outcome and/or Purpose	The regional knowledge and support technical assistance (TA) supports the implementation of a pilot cross-border economic corridor around Almaty and Bishkek under the Central Asia Regional Economic Cooperation (CAREC) program. The Almaty–Bishkek Economic Corridor (ABEC, the corridor) follows a multisector approach to create one economic space without barriers. ABEC will allow businesses to specialize more, operate at a larger scale and achieve greater diversification and competitiveness with the purpose of exporting goods and services outside the region.
Expected Results	The regional TA will identify investment projects for ADB, the governments, the private sector, and other development partners through the platform of the corridor. The TA will also actively promote private sector investments in the corridor, support the further institutionalization of ABEC, and assist the ABEC subcommittee in identifying, prioritizing, and sequencing ABEC projects and reform initiatives.

2020 Committed Projects

ADB Approved Number	Project Name
TA 6535-REG	Addressing Health Threats in Central Asia Regional Economic Cooperation Countries and the Caucasus
TA 6589-REG	Supporting Economic Corridor Development in Armenia and Georgia to Enhance Trade and Competitiveness
TA 9968-REG	Preparing Projects to Enhance Transport Connectivity and Resilience in the Pacific
TA 6528-REG	Strengthening the Implementation of Regional Cooperation and Integration Initiatives of South Asian Association for Regional Cooperation
TA 9971-REG	Southeast Asia Agriculture, Natural Resources, and Rural Development Facility Phase II
TA 6542-TIM	Capacity for Multilateral and Regional Economic Integration
TA 6561-REG	Strengthening the Enabling Environment for Disaster Risk Financing (Phase 2)
TA 6628-REG	Promoting Innovations in Regional Cooperation and Integration in the Aftermath of COVID-19
TA 6660-PRC	Enhancing the Sustainable Cooperation of Yunnan and Guizhou with the Greater Mekong Subregion
TA 6687-PRC	Supporting Sustainable Finance and Regional Cooperation
TA 9630-REG	Assessing Economic Corridor Development Potential Among Kazakhstan, Uzbekistan, and Tajikistan
TA 9709-REG	Regional Cooperation on Increasing Cross-Border Energy Trading within the Central Asian Power System–Modernization of Coordinating Dispatch Center Energiya (Subproject 1)
TA 9916-REG	Greater Mekong Subregion Sustainable Agriculture and Food Security Program
TA 6591-REG	Enhancing Road Safety for Central Asia Regional Economic Cooperation Member Countries (Phase 2)

COVID-19 = coronavirus disease, REG = regional, SDTC-RCI = Regional Cooperation and Integration Thematic Group of the Sustainable Development and Climate Change Department, TIM = Timor-Leste.

7 INVESTMENT CLIMATE FACILITATION FUND under the REGIONAL COOPERATION AND INTEGRATION FINANCING FACILITY (RCIFPF-ICFF)

Donor: Japan

Year Established	2008
Financing Products	Technical Assistance (TA)
Objective	The objective of ICFF is to promote investments in ADB's developing member countries (DMCs) and facilitate regional cooperation and integration (RCI) through the construction of basic infrastructure, improvements in the investment climate, capacity building, and promotion of good governance, among others.
Eligible Sectors	Funding priority will be given to projects that promote financial sector development and regional investment. Examples are projects that aim to improve financial regulatory and supervisory frameworks, mitigate risks in financial markets, harmonize regional investment policies, and streamline procedures for investment applications and approvals.
Facility Manager	Ronald Antonio Q. Butiong, Chief of Regional Cooperation and Integration Thematic Group, SDTC-RCI
Alternate Facility Managers	Yuebin Zhang, Principal Regional Cooperation Specialist, SDTC-RCI Hiroki Kasahara, Principal Financing Partnerships Specialist, SDPF

Financial Position as of 31 December 2020
(Amount in $ million)

Cumulative Donor Commitment	Net Balance Available for Trust Fund Committee Allocation		Number of Projects Funded (Approvals)	Number of Projects Funded (Commitments)
Amount	Amount	% of Commitment		
31.54	3.2	10%	30	30

Featured Project

TA 9404-REG: Supporting the Development of Asian Bond Markets through AsianBondsOnline	
Committed Amount	$1.5 million financed by ICFF
Commitment Date	17 October 2017
Completion Date	31 December 2020
Outcome and/or Purpose	The knowledge and support TA will strengthen, broaden, and sustain growth of Asian bond markets by disseminating information on the region's bond markets, creating knowledge products, and engaging in capacity building activities. The activities are expected to contribute to more informed and better functioning bond markets that lead to increased regional monetary and financial cooperation and integration in the Association of Southeast Asian Nations (ASEAN)+3. All activities will be undertaken in support of the Asian Bond Markets Initiative (ABMI), including its medium-term road map that was approved in May 2016. The TA is relevant to Strategy 2030, which indicates ADB's support for private sector development, including mobilizing private resources for development highlighting the importance of strengthening Asian bond markets.

TA 9404-REG: Supporting the Development of Asian Bond Markets through AsianBondsOnline	
Results	The AsianBondsOnline (ABO) website revamp was completed, and the new ABO website was launched online on 3 July 2018. Nine issues of Asia Bond Monitor had been published and disseminated, five of which were launched in Kuala Lumpur, Malaysia; Seoul, the Republic of Korea; Singapore; Ha Noi, Viet Nam; and Phnom Penh, Cambodia. Bond market studies were completed and disseminated on the factors driving foreign and domestic investments in bond markets, the role of greenness in green bond pricing, the impact of the Asian Bond Markets Initiative on bond market development in Asia, importance of developing the housing bond market, and the effect of bond market development on banks' risk taking. Two capacity building workshops were held, in 2018 and 2019. For 2018, the workshop was held in Vientiane, Lao People's Democratic Republic on 9–10 August and participated by more than 70 officials from public and private sectors. For 2019, the workshop was organized in Ho Chi Minh City, Viet Nam on 27 September and participated by over 100 participants both from the public and private sectors. Regional bond market development experiences, thematic issues in bond market developments, economic outlook, and regional bond market development were discussed.

2020 Committed Projects

ADB Approved Number	Project Name
TA 6592-REG	Building Financial Resilience and Stability to Reinvigorate Growth
TA 9957-REG	Enhance AsianBondsOnline as the Primary Bond Information Platform in ASEAN+3
TA 6641-REG	Support for ASEAN+3 Bond Market Forum under the Asian Bond Markets Initiative Medium-Term Road Map, 2019–2022

ASEAN = Association of Southeast Asian Nations, REG = regional, SDPF = Partner Funds Division of the Sustainable Development and Climate Change Department, SDTC-RCI = Regional Cooperation and Integration Thematic Group of the Sustainable Development and Climate Change Department.

8 UNITED KINGDOM FUND FOR ASIA REGIONAL TRADE AND CONNECTIVITY under the REGIONAL COOPERATION AND INTEGRATION FINANCING PARTNERSHIP FACILITY (RCIFPF–ARTCF)

Donors: The United Kingdom and Northern Ireland (acting through DFID)

Year Established	2018
Financing Products	Technical Assistance (TA)
Objective	The ARTCF aims to support the implementation of ADB's Operational Plan for Regional Cooperation and Integration, 2016–2020 (RCI-OP) by financing regional cooperation and integration (RCI) activities in selected developing member countries (DMCs) in Asia covering Central, South, and Southeast Asia, leading to improved integration with other regions of the world.
Eligible Sectors	The ARTCF will support RCI activities in the following sectors and/or areas: (i) regional electricity connectivity and trade, (ii) transport connectivity, (iii) digital connectivity, (iv) regulatory reform and broad regional trade and investment facilitation, (v) regional and/or cross-border value chains, and (vi) broader strategic issues related to connectivity investments.
Facility Manager	Ronald Antonio Q. Butiong, Chief of Regional Cooperation and Integration Thematic Group, SDTC-RCI
Alternate Facility Manager	Ashish Narain, Principal Economist, PASP

Financial Position as of 31 December 2020
(Amount in $ million)

Cumulative Donor Commitment	Net Balance Available for Trust Fund Committee Allocation		Number of Projects Funded (Approvals)	Number of Projects Funded (Commitments)
Amount	Amount	% of Commitment		
28.90[1]	6.3	22%	14	14

Featured Project

TA 9641-REG: Railway Sector Development in Central Asia Regional Economic Cooperation Countries	
Committed Amount	$2 million of which $1 million is financed by ARTCF
Commitment Date	14 November 2018
Expected Completion Date	31 December 2022
Expected Outcome and/or Purpose	The knowledge and support TA will accelerate the sound development of the railway subsector in Central Asia Regional Economic Cooperation (CAREC) countries through (i) railway transport market research, (ii) project identification and preparation, (iii) knowledge sharing, and (iv) capacity development. The TA supports regional and interregional trade and cooperation and promotes ADB as a prime development partner in the railway subsector in Central and West Asia, aiming for strong, long-term engagement with CAREC member countries.

---

[1] Figure includes revaluation and devaluation of contributions not yet remitted to ADB at reporting period.

TA 9641-REG: Railway Sector Development in Central Asia Regional Economic Cooperation Countries

Expected Results	The TA is expected to (i) develop a regional transport model that will indicate main traffic flows by origin and destination and type of cargo; (ii) facilitate swift mobilization of expertise to screen project options, perform prefeasibility studies or validate existing pre-feasibility or feasibility studies, and support the prioritization and initial conceptualization of investments; (iii) develop knowledge products and conduct events in common areas of interest in sector reform and commercialization; and (iv) facilitate activities to strengthen the capacity of railway agencies in key areas required for the development of bankable projects.
	In 2020, the TA has resulted in (i) development of a CAREC Transportation Model, (ii) publication on track capacity and timetabling software (in response to a request of the CAREC Railway Working Group), and (iii) preparation of 11 country rail sector assessment reports.

2020 Committed Projects

ADB Approved Number	Project Name
TA 9487-REG	Almaty–Bishkek Economic Corridor Support
TA 6579-REG	"Early Harvest" Implementation of the Cross-Border Transport and Trade Facilitation in the Greater Mekong Subregion
TA 6540-REG	Fostering Expanded Regional Electricity and Gas Interconnection and Trade under the CAREC Energy Strategy 2030
TA 9420-REG	Implementation of Sustainable Transport For All (Supplementary)
TA 6628-REG	Promoting Innovations in Regional Cooperation and Integration in the Aftermath of COVID-19
TA 6558-REG	Strengthening Knowledge and Capacities for the Design and Implementation of Free Trade Agreements Involving Central Asia Regional Economic Cooperation Countries

COVID-19 = coronavirus disease, DFID = Department for International Development, PASP = Social Sectors and Public Sector Management Division of the Pacific Department, REG = regional, SDTC-RCI = Regional Cooperation and Integration Thematic Group of the Sustainable Development and Climate Change Department.

9 ASEAN AUSTRALIA SMART CITIES TRUST FUND under the URBAN FINANCING PARTNERSHIP FACILITY (UFPF–AASCTF)

Donor: Government of Australia's Department of Foreign Affairs and Trade

Year Established	2019
Financing Products	Grant, Technical Assistance (TA)
Objective	The envisioned impact of the fund is aligned with ADB's Strategy 2030 which includes an operational focus on building livable cities that are green, competitive, inclusive, and resilient, and Association of Southeast Asian Nations Sustainable Urbanization Strategy which aims to promote high quality of life, competitive economies, and sustainable environments.
Eligible Sectors	Water and Other Urban Infrastructure Services
Facility Manager **Alternate Facility Manager**	Robert Guild, Chief Sector Officer, SDSC Manoj Sharma, Chief of Urban Sector Group, SDSC-URB

Financial Position as of 31 December 2020
(Amount in $ million)

Cumulative Donor Commitment	Net Balance Available for Trust Fund Committee Allocation		Number of Projects Funded (Approvals)	Number of Projects Funded (Commitments)
Amount	Amount	% of Commitment		
14.60	3.9	27%	1	1

Featured Project

TA 9554-REG: Southeast Asia Urban Services Facility	
Committed Amount	$10 million
Commitment Date	18 September 2019
Expected Completion Date	30 June 2024
Expected Outcome and/or Purpose	The TA facility will support the delivery of solutions for (i) tackling climate change, building climate and disaster resilience, and enhancing environmental sustainability; (ii) making cities more livable; and (iii) strengthening governance and institutional capacity.
Expected Results	The TA outputs include (i) improved planning, project design, and readiness; (ii) improved developing member country staff capacity in project administration and urban service delivery; and (iii) improved knowledge management and sharing among Southeast Asia developing member countries.

REG = regional, SDSC = Office of the Cluster Head of the Sustainable Development and Climate Change Department, SDSC-URB = Urban Sector Group of the Sustainable Development and Climate Change Department.

2020 Committed Direct Charges

Project Name
Livable Cities Forum on Digital Solutions

10 CITIES DEVELOPMENT INITIATIVE FOR ASIA TRUST FUND under the URBAN FINANCING PARTNERSHIP FACILITY (UFPF–CDIATF)

Donors: Governments of Austria, Germany, and Switzerland

Year Established	2017
Financing Products	Technical Assistance (TA)
Objective	To assist secondary cities in developing member countries (DMCs) in preparing sustainable and bankable urban infrastructure projects, linking them with funding sources, and strengthening their capacities to develop and implement high priority investments.
Eligible Sectors	Water and Other Urban Infrastructure
Facility Manager	Robert Guild, Chief Sector Officer, SDSC

Financial Position as of 31 December 2020
(Amount in $ million)

Cumulative Donor Commitment	Net Balance Available for Trust Fund Committee Allocation		Number of Projects Funded (Approvals)	Number of Projects Funded (Commitments)
Amount	Amount	% of Commitment		
9.20	1.4	15%	2	2

Featured Projects

TA 6559-REG: Implementing the Cities Development Initiative for Asia	
Committed Amount	$4,500,000
Commitment Date	8 September 2020
Expected Completion Date	31 December 2023
Expected Outcome and/or Purpose	Financing for inclusive and gender-responsive investments in cities in DMCs is increased.
Expected Results	(i) At least $1 billion in new financing generated for investments in Cities Development Initiative for Asia project cities by 2023. (ii) At least six completed project preparation studies financed by development partners, governments, or the private sector by 2023.

TA 8556-REG: Supporting the Cities Development Initiative for Asia	
Committed Amount	$3,094,889
Commitment Date	22 May 2019
Expected Completion Date	31 December 2020
Expected Outcome and/or Purpose	ADB urban infrastructure investment projects supported by prefeasibility studies
Expected Results	At least seven ADB urban infrastructure projects designed with project prefeasibility study support by 2020.

REG = regional, SDSC = Office of the Cluster Head of the Sustainable Development and Climate Change Department.

2020 Committed Projects

ADB Approved Number	Project Name
TA 6559	Implementing the Cities Development Initiative for Asia

11 URBAN ENVIRONMENTAL INFRASTRUCTURE FUND under the URBAN FINANCING PARTNERSHIP FACILITY (UFPF–UEIF)

Donor: Sweden

Year Established	2009
Financing Products	Grant, Technical Assistance, Direct Charge
Objective	Support city-level engagement to build resilience to climate change and impact positively upon the vulnerability of the urban poor.
Eligible Sectors	Multisector
Facility Manager Alternate Facility Manager	Robert Guild, Chief Sector Officer, SDSC Manoj Sharma, Chief of Urban Sector Group, SDSC-URB

Financial Position as of 31 December 2020
(Amount in $ million)

Cumulative Donor Commitment	Net Balance Available for Trust Fund Committee Allocation		Number of Projects Funded (Approvals)	Number of Projects Funded (Commitments)
Amount	Amount	% of Commitment		
21.45	0.5	2%	25	25

Featured Projects

Loan 3098/3099; Grant 0380-MON: Ulaanbaatar Urban Services and *Ger* Areas Development Investment Program—Tranche 1	
Committed Amount	$3.7 million
Commitment Date	30 June 2014
Completion Date	21 November 2019 (financial closure)
Outcome and/or Purpose	Improve operational efficiency of water service providers or utilities in selected *ger* area subcenters
Results	Optimized and integrated management of Ulaanbaatar's water supply system through plant equipment upgrading for transmission lines and water treatment facilities, installation of a fiber optic connectivity network, installation of a supervisory control and data acquisition system, installation of monitoring wells, and establishment of the Water Supply and Sewerage Authority surveillance and control center that will help improve the provision of water and wastewater services to the citizens of the city.

Loan 2983; Grant 0334-CAM: Greater Mekong Subregion Southern Economic Corridor Towns Development Project – Mainstreaming 3R Approach	
Committed Amount	$1.5 million
Commitment Date	17 January 2013
Completion Date	30 June 2019 (financial closure)
Outcome and/or Purpose	Urban infrastructure improved and climate resilience enhanced in Battambang, Bavet, and Poipet
Results	Completed the construction of materials recovery facilities for the towns of Battambang, Bavet, and Poipet to that will form part of the other investments on solid waste management in these towns which is expected to help improve not only their urban environmental conditions but also enhance their potential as agro-industrial and/or tourism hubs in the country.

2020 Committed Direct Charges

Project Name
KAZ: Preparing a National Feasibility Study for Nur-Sultan Wastewater Treatment Plant

3R = reduce, reuse, recycle; CAM = Cambodia; KAZ = Kazakhstan; MON = Mongolia, SDSC = Office of the Cluster Head of the Sustainable Development and Climate Change Department, SDSC-URB = Urban Sector Group of the Sustainable Development and Climate Change Department.

12 URBAN CLIMATE CHANGE RESILIENCE TRUST FUND under the URBAN FINANCING PARTNERSHIP FACILITY (UFPF–UCCRTF)

Donors: The Rockefeller Foundation, Switzerland, and the United Kingdom

Year Established	2013
Financing Products	Grant, Technical Assistance (TA)
Objective	To help 25 fast-growing cities in Asia to reduce risks poor people face from floods, storms, and extreme climate events, by helping to better plan and design infrastructure to invest against these impacts.
Eligible Sectors	Water and Other Urban Infrastructure Services
Facility Manager **Alternate Facility Manager**	Robert Guild, Chief Sector Officer, SDSC Manoj Sharma, Chief of Urban Sector Group, SDSC-URB

Financial Position as of 31 December 2020
(Amount in $ million)

Cumulative Donor Commitment	Net Balance Available for Trust Fund Committee Allocation		Number of Projects Funded (Approvals)	Number of Projects Funded (Commitments)
Amount	Amount	% of Commitment		
144.50	20.8	14%	41[2]	41

Featured Project

TA 9660-REG: Promoting Transformative Gender Equality Agenda in Asia and the Pacific	
Committed Amount	$735,000
Commitment Date	9 July 2020
Expected Completion Date	31 December 2025
Expected Outcome and/or Purpose	(i) Operations at local government level in at least two cities utilize guidelines on gender-responsive climate-resilient urban planning and governance. (ii) Proactive and transformative gender design features strengthened in at least two operations. (iii) Women's leadership and decision-making in urban governance enhanced.
Expected Results	(i) Knowledge and capacity of city government stakeholders and women leaders in gender-responsive climate-resilient urban planning and governance strengthened. (ii) Knowledge of urban stakeholders in the use of financial instruments for women's disaster resilience increased.

---

2   UCCRTF has 23 direct charges in addition to the 41 approved and committed projects.

2020 Committed Projects and Direct Charges

Projects

ADB Approved Number	Project Name
TA 9829-IND	Strengthening Climate Change Resilience in Urban India–Strengthening Smart Urban Mass Rapid Transit and Climate Change Resilience in the National Capital Region (Subproject 3)
TA 9960-REG	Integrated High Impact Innovation in Sustainable Energy Technology: Pilot Testing of Innovative Energy Technologies and Business Models (Subproject 3)
TA 9660-REG	Promoting Transformative Gender Equality Agenda in Asia and the Pacific (Supplementary)

Direct Charges

Project Name
UCCRDC00027 BAN: United Delcot Water Limited: Preparing the Purbachal Water Distribution Network Project

BAN = Bangladesh, IND = India, REG = regional, SDSC = Office of the Cluster Head of the Sustainable Development and Climate Change Department, SDSC-URB = Urban Sector Group of the Sustainable Development and Climate Change Department.

13 NETHERLANDS TRUST FUND
under the WATER FINANCING PARTNERSHIP FACILITY (WFPF-NET)

Donor: The Netherlands

Year Established	2007
Financing Products	Technical Assistance (TA), Grant, Direct Charge
Objective	The WFPF is supporting the implementation of ADB's water financing program 2006–2020 and Water Operational Plan 2011–2020 aimed at doubling ADB's annual water investment to well over $2 billion or at least $30 billion from 2006 to 2020. Moving forward after 2020, WFPF will support the implementation of ADB's water operations under Strategy 2030 guided by the Water Sector Framework 2021–2030: Water-Secure and Resilient Asia-Pacific currently under preparation which will cover the following focal areas: (i) water as a sustainable resource, (ii) universal and safe water services, (iii) productive water in agriculture and energy, and (iv) reduced water-related disaster risks. The fund prioritizes activities designed to result in significantly more people with access to safe drinking water and improved sanitation, higher productivity and efficiency of irrigation and drainage services, more people with reduced risk of flooding; sustainable management of water resources; increased knowledge and capacity; improved sector governance; and increased focus on water-food security nexus.
Eligible Sectors	Agriculture, Natural Resources, and Rural Development; Water and Other Urban Infrastructure and Services
Facility Manager **Alternate Facility Manager**	Robert Guild, Chief Sector Officer, SDSC Christian Walder (Acting), Water Supply and Sanitation Specialist, SDSC-WAT

Financial Position as of 31 December 2020
(Amount in $ million)

Cumulative Donor Commitment	Net Balance Available for Trust Fund Committee Allocation		Number of Projects Funded (Approvals)	Number of Projects Funded (Commitments)
Amount	Amount	% of Commitment		
44.24	1.7	4%	31[3]	31[3]

Featured Project

TA 6568: Implementation Support for the Priority River Basins Flood Risk Management Project	
Commitment Amount	$750,000 WFPF-cofinancing of TA attached to loan
Committed Date	23 October 2020 (TA attached to loan signing date) 22 December 2020 (loan signing date)
Expected Completion Date	30 September 2023 (TA attached to loan closing date) 30 September 2027 (loan closing date)

[3]   Excludes direct charges.

TA 6568: Implementation Support for the Priority River Basins Flood Risk Management Project

Expected Outcome and/or Purpose	The project will improve the resilience of communities to flooding in six river basins in the Terai region by constructing flood embankments, spurs, and outlet structures, including planning and implementation of bioengineering of river embankments for enhanced flood risk management, using suitable vegetative methods to prevent soil erosion. It will support the development of maintenance manuals and asset management system for flood protection infrastructure. The local response to flooding will be strengthened through the installation of flood forecasting and early warning systems (FFEWS) and community-based disaster risk management.
Expected Results	Improved resilience of communities to flood risks in the six river basins in the Terai region with (i) 2,300 hectares of agricultural land and 2,850 households protected from 1-in-50-year flooding, and (ii) daily river flow information displayed on the Department of Hydrology and Meteorology river watch system, and flood risk bulletin based on FFEWS forecasts disseminated to communities and relevant agencies in line with Nepal's standard operating procedures.

2020 Committed Projects and Direct Charges

Projects

ADB Approved Number	Project Name
TA9323	TRTA-LAO: Sustainable Rural Infrastructure and Watershed Management Sector Facility–Preparation of the That Luang Marsh Fishway
TA6546	TRTA-BAN: Climate-Resilient Livelihood Improvement and Watershed Management in Chittagong Hill Tracts Project
TA9442	TRTA-PAK: Khyber Pakhtunkhwa Water Resources Development Project
TA9443	TRTA-REG: Strengthening Capacity to Design and Implement Water and Rural Infrastructure Facility (Nepal: Preparing Mechanized Irrigation Innovation Project)
TA6663	KSTA-PAK: Strengthening Food Security Post COVID-19 and Locust Attack
TA6568	TA Attached to Loan-NEP: Implementation Support for the Priority River Basins Flood Risk Management Project
TA 9927	TRTA-BAN: Climate and Disaster Resilient Small-Scale Water Resources Management Project

Direct Charges

Project Name
IND: Irrigation Scheduling through Remote Sensing-Based Water Consumption Management–Support to Implementation of Madhya Pradesh Efficiency Irrigation Investment Project
PAK: Support to Preparation of Water Resources Management Investment Projects in Sindh Province
INO: Support to Water and Food Security Planning and Investment through Earth Observation Services
PAK: Support to Preparation of Thal Canal Irrigation Project

BAN = Bangladesh, IND = India, KSTA = knowledge and support technical assistance, LAO = Lao People's Democratic Republic, NEP = Nepal, PAK = Pakistan, REG = regional, SDSC = Office of the Cluster Head of the Sustainable Development and Climate Change Department, SDSC-WAT = Water Sector Group of the Sustainable Development and Climate Change Department, TRTA = transaction technical assistance.

14 MULTI-DONOR TRUST FUND
under the WATER FINANCING PARTNERSHIP FACILITY (WFPF-MPTF)

Donors: Australia, Austria, Norway,[4] Spain, and Switzerland[5]

Year Established	2006
Financing Products	Technical Assistance (TA), Grant, Direct Charge
Objective	The WFPF is supporting the implementation of ADB's water financing program 2006–2020 and Water Operational Plan 2011–2020 aimed at doubling ADB's annual water investment to well over $2 billion or at least $30 billion from 2006 to 2020. Moving forward after 2020, WFPF will support the implementation of ADB's water operations under Strategy 2030 guided by the Water Sector Framework 2021-2030: Water-Secure and Resilient Asia-Pacific currently under preparation which will cover the following focal areas: (i) water as a sustainable resource, (ii) universal and safe water services, (iii) productive water in agriculture and energy, and (iv) reduced water-related disaster risks. The fund prioritizes activities designed to result in significantly more people with access to safe drinking water and improved sanitation, higher productivity and efficiency of irrigation and drainage services, more people with reduced risk of flooding; sustainable management of water resources; increased knowledge and capacity; and improved sector governance.
Eligible Sectors	Water and Other Urban Infrastructure and Services; Agriculture, Natural Resources, and Rural Development
Facility Manager **Alternate Facility Manager**	Robert Guild, Chief Sector Officer, SDSC Christian Walder (Acting), Water Supply and Sanitation Specialist, SDSC-WAT

Financial Position as of 31 December 2020
(Amount in $ million)

Cumulative Donor Commitment	Net Balance Available for Trust Fund Committee Allocation		Number of Projects Funded (Approvals)	Number of Projects Funded (Commitments)
Amount	**Amount**	**% of Commitment**		
52.37	0.8	1%	100[6]	100[6]

Featured Project

TRTA 9200: Preparing South Tarawa Water Supply Project	
Committed Amount	$150,000 WFPF TRTA Cofinancing
Commitment Date	6 November 2020 (grant signing date)
Expected Completion Date	31 December 2027 (grant closing date date)

---

[4] Norway was part of the Multi-Donor Trust Fund from 2007 to 2017.
[5] Switzerland was part of the Multi-Donor Trust Fund from 2012 to 2020.
[6] Excludes direct charges.

TRTA 9200: Preparing South Tarawa Water Supply Project	
Expected Outcome and/or Purpose	The project will combat factors that result in the high incidence of waterborne disease in Kiribati's capital, South Tarawa, through the delivery and effective management of new and rehabilitated climate-resilient water supply assets and of improved hygiene practices. Climate-resilient and low-carbon water supply infrastructure Capacity of Ministry of Infrastructure and Sustainable Energy and Public Utilities Board to effectively manage water supply infrastructure increased. This will be delivered through 5-year operation and maintenance contracts for the desalination plant and water supply network. Awareness of water, sanitation, and hygiene (WASH) and climate change issues is raised. This will be achieved through the implementation of a 5-year WASH and climate change awareness program.
Expected Results	Increased access of 95% of South Tarawa's population (51.5% women) to safe, climate-resilient water supplies by 2027.

2020 Committed Project

ADB Approved Number	Project Name
TA 9971	TRTA-REG: Southeast Asia Agriculture, Natural Resources, and Rural Development Facility–Phase II

REG = regional, SDSC = Office of the Cluster Head of the Sustainable Development and Climate Change Department, SDSC-WAT = Water Sector Group of the Sustainable Development and Climate Change Department, TRTA = transaction technical assistance.

15 SANITATION FINANCING PARTNERSHIP TRUST FUND under the WATER FINANCING PARTNERSHIP FACILITY (WFPF–SFPTF)

Donor: Bill & Melinda Gates Foundation

Year Established	2013
Financing Products	Technical Assistance (TA), Grant, Direct Charge
Objective	The WFPF is supporting the implementation of ADB's water financing program 2006–2020 and Water Operational Plan 2011–2020 aimed at doubling ADB's annual water investment to well over $2 billion or at least $30 billion from 2006 to 2020. Moving forward after 2020, WFPF will support the implementation of ADB's water operations under Strategy 2030 guided by the Water Sector Framework 2021–2030: Water-Secure and Resilient Asia and the Pacific currently under preparation which will cover the following focal areas: (i) water as a sustainable resource, (ii) universal and safe water services, (iii) productive water in agriculture and energy, and (iv) reduced water-related disaster risks. The fund initially focused on innovative sanitation solutions to increase support for fecal sludge management through non-networked (non-sewered) sanitation and septage management. The focus has now shifted to a more holistic approach through the citywide inclusive sanitation framework to increase access to appropriate sanitation systems, whether sewered or non-sewered, centralized or decentralized, including the required support to increase knowledge and capacity and improve governance.
Eligible Sectors	Water and Other Urban Infrastructure and Services
Facility Manager **Alternate Facility Manager**	Robert Guild, Chief Sector Officer, SDSC Christian Walder (Acting), Water Supply and Sanitation Specialist, SDSC-WAT

Financial Position as of 31 December 2020
(Amount in $ million)

Cumulative Donor Commitment	Net Balance Available for Trust Fund Committee Allocation		Number of Projects Funded (Approvals)	Number of Projects Funded (Commitments)
Amount	Amount	% of Commitment		
19.00	0.4	2%	16[7]	16[7]

Featured Project

TRTA 9753-PRC: Preparing Environmental and Rural Development Projects (Hunan Miluo River Disaster Risk Management and Comprehensive Environment Improvement Project)	
Committed Amount	$150,000 WFPF TRTA Cofinancing
Commitment Date	27 November 2020 (loan approval date)
Expected Completion Date	30 November 2027 (loan closing date)

---

[7] Excludes direct charges.

TRTA 9753-PRC: Preparing Environmental and Rural Development Projects (Hunan Miluo River Disaster Risk Management and Comprehensive Environment Improvement Project)

Expected Outcome and/or Purpose	The project will promote rural vitalization and ecological protection by (i) instituting and applying international best practices for flood and integrated disaster risk management, (ii) improving access to safe drinking water and sanitation services for urban and rural residents, (iii) promoting circular agricultural development by linking sustainable livestock waste management and eco-farming, (iv) piloting green procurement practices and mainstreaming environmental education, and (v) enhancing institutional coordination capacity to maximize the project's impact.
Expected Results	A total of 523,333 residents of 239 villages in 25 project towns and subdistricts in Pingjiang County benefitted through (i) reduced impact of flooding and flood disaster-related losses, (ii) improved access to safe drinking water and sanitation services, (iii) increased crop yields and farmers' agricultural incomes, and (iv) reduced health risks through improved environment and sanitation.

2020 Committed Projects

ADB Approved Number	Project Name
TA 9732-PRC	Preparing Urban and Social Development Projects
TA 9753-PRC	Preparing Environmental and Rural Development Projects (Supplementary)

PRC = People's Republic of China, SDSC = Office of the Cluster Head of the Sustainable Development and Climate Change Department, SDSC-WAT = Water Sector Group of the Sustainable Development and Climate Change Department, TRTA = transaction technical assistance.

16 · ADB VENTURES INVESTMENT FUND 1 under the ADB VENTURES FINANCING PARTNERSHIP FACILITY (VIF1)

Donors: Clean Technology Fund, Finland, the Republic of Korea, Korea Venture Investment Corporation, NDF

Year Established	2020
Financing Products	Equity Investments
Objective	Investing in early-stage technology companies contributing to the Sustainable Development Goals with a focus on climate and gender impact.
Eligible Sectors	Cleantech, Agritech, Healthtech, Fintech
Fund Manager	Dominic Mellor, Principal Investment Specialist, OPSD

Financial Position as of 31 December 2020
(Amount in $ million)

Cumulative Donor Commitment	Net Balance Available for Trust Fund Committee Allocation		Number of Projects Funded	Number of Projects Funded
Amount	Amount	% of Commitment	(Approvals)	(Commitments)
59.65[8]	–	–	1	NA

– = Net available balance is commercially sensitive information and cannot be disclosed to the public.
OPSD = Office of the Director General of the Private Sector Operations Department.

---

[8] Cumulative donor commitment amount here is shown as US$ equivalent Donor Commitment, still inclusive of foreign exchange adjustment. Actual net cumulative donor commitment received amounts to $59.29 million.

17 AFGHANISTAN INFRASTRUCTURE TRUST FUND (AITF)

Donors: Afghan National Army (ANA) Trust Fund, Canada, Germany, Japan, the United Kingdom, and the United States

Year Established	2010
Financing Products	Grant, Technical Assistance (TA)
Objective	To pool and deliver financing for infrastructure development in Afghanistan and to leverage resources through cofinancing with private sector and other development partners. The fund will provide grant cofinancing alongside ADB-funded infrastructure projects, with resources supplementing those provided by ADB through its own operational budget. ADB will provide operational and project management expertise to enable the Afghanistan government to implement the country's key infrastructure development plans. The Afghanistan Ministry of Finance and ADB will work together to ensure that the fund is efficiently utilized to support the highest priority infrastructure projects and leverage additional financing from the private sector and other partners.
Eligible Sectors	Agriculture and Natural Resources, Energy, Transport, Water, and Urban
Fund Manager **Alternate Fund Manager**	Narendra Singru, Country Director, AFRM Artur Andrysiak, Deputy Country Director, AFRM

Financial Position as of 31 December 2020
(Amount in $ million)

Cumulative Donor Commitment	Net Balance Available for Trust Fund Committee Allocation		Number of Projects Funded	Number of Projects Funded
Amount	**Amount**	**% of Commitment**	(Approvals)	(Commitments)
773.2	195.0[9]	26%	19	19

Featured Project

Grant 0556-AFG: Energy Supply Investment Program—Tranche 4	
Committed Amount	$60 million
Commitment Date	17 October 2017
Expected Completion Date	30 June 2023
Expected Outcome and/or Purpose	The project will finance the northeast power grid extension through construction of a 220-kilovolt (kV) transmission line from Kabul to Jalalabad province, and construction of a 220/110 kV substation in Jalalabad. It will extend the national grid into the eastern provinces with a population of nearly 2 million people.

---

[9] The funds available under the AITF are already marked for two projects: (i) $143.80 million from the Afghanistan National Army Trust Fund ($45.00 million), the United States Agency for International Development ($18.00 million), and German development cooperation through KfW ($80.77 million) for the Energy Sector Stand Alone Project which is firm for 2021; and (ii) $46.00 million from the Government of Japan for Transport Network Improvement Project (Kabul–Jalalabad Road) which is firm for 2022.

Grant 0556-AFG: Energy Supply Investment Program—Tranche 4

Expected Results	The project will allow (i) transmission of domestic power generation and extension of the power interconnection to the country's eastern load centers, (ii) interconnection of isolated networks into a unified grid, and (iii) greater power system stability. The project will also provide sustainable power to two industrial parks in the east and enable grid stability by interconnecting transmission lines in the adjoining provinces. The transmission line will have the capacity to transmit 300 megawatts of power and energize an additional 300,000 new connections to residential, commercial, and industrial consumers.

2020 Committed Projects

ADB Approved Number	Project Name
Grant 0770-AFG	Energy Supply Investment Program—Tranche 7
TA 6664-AFG	Natural Resources Operations Support and Enhancement

AFG = Afghanistan, AFRM = Afghanistan Resident Mission of the Central and West Asia Department.

18 ASIA-PACIFIC CLIMATE FINANCE FUND (ACliFF)

Donor: Germany

Year Established	2017
Financing Products	Grant, Technical Assistance (TA), Direct Charge
Objective	Support the identification, development, and implementation of financial risk management products that can help mitigate and manage a range of climate investment and/or extreme weather risks associated with sovereign and nonsovereign investments wholly or partially focused on climate change mitigation, adaptation and/or disaster risk management.
Eligible Sectors	Multisector
Fund Manager Alternate Fund Manager	Joshua Ling, Climate Change Specialist, SDCD Charlotte Benson, Principal Disaster Risk Management Specialist, SDCD

Financial Position as of 31 December 2020
(Amount in $ million)

Cumulative Donor Commitment	Net Balance Available for Trust Fund Committee Allocation		Number of Projects Funded (Approvals)	Number of Projects Funded (Commitments)
Amount	**Amount**	**% of Commitment**		
33.80	9.32	28%	5[10]	5[10]

Featured Project

TA 9948-REG: ADB Ventures	
Committed Amount	$1,400,000
Commitment Date	29 September 2020
Expected Completion Date	31 December 2022
Expected Outcome and/or Purpose	To support early-stage companies with technology-enabled solutions to test new products, business models, and to scale their impact, contributing to the Sustainable Development Goals (SDGs) in ADB's developing member countries (DMCs), including SDG 13. Supported start-ups utilize technology to develop climate-related financial risk management solutions.
Expected Results	To enable the growth of early-stage companies providing climate-focused financial risk management related technology solutions: (i) supporting the mobilization of additional investments; and (ii) expanding the number of individuals benefiting from the solutions provided.

---

[10] Includes three Direct Charges.

2020 Committed Projects and Direct Charges

Projects

ADB Approved Number	Project Name
TA 9766-REG	Southeast Asia Public Management, Financial Sector, and Trade Policy Facility (Supplementary)
TA 9948-REG	ADB Ventures Technical Assistance (Supplementary)

Direct Charges

Project Name
Pacific DMCs: Pacific Renewable Energy Project (PREP)
UZB: Partial Credit Guarantee Facility for Uzbekistan Solar Public–Private Partnerships (PPP) Program
KAZ: Green Investment Finance Project (KGIFP)

ADB = Asian Development Bank, KAZ = Kazakhstan, REG = regional, SDCD = Climate Change and Disaster Risk Management Division of the Sustainable Development and Climate Change Department, UZB = Uzbekistan.

19 ASIA PACIFIC PROJECT PREPARATION FACILITY (AP3F)

Donors: Australia, Canada, and Japan

Year Established	2014
Financing Products	Grant, Technical Assistance, Direct Charge
Objective	The fund is to provide financial assistance to developing member countries' governments and their public sector agencies to support the financial, legal, and technical advisory services required to prepare and structure transactions. The fund also offers support for enabling reforms and capacity building that can be linked to potential or current transactions.
Eligible Sectors	All sectors
Facility Manager Alternate Facility Manager	Yoji Morishita, Head, OPPP Ichiro Aoki – AP3F Secretariat, Senior Public-Private Partnership Specialist, OPOH

Financial Position as of 31 December 2020
(Amount in $ million)

Cumulative Donor Commitment	Net Balance Available for Trust Fund Committee Allocation		Number of Projects Funded (Approvals)	Number of Projects Funded (Commitments)
Amount	Amount	% of Commitment		
63.3	31	49%	1[11]	1[11]

Featured Project

AP3F053/PP020: UZB: Second Phase - Sherabad Solar Independent Power Producer (IPP) in the Surkhandarya Region	
Committed Amount	$725,325
Commitment Date	1 October 2020
Expected Completion Date	31 December 2021
Expected Outcome and/or Purpose	The purpose of the support is to assist in the project preparation and tendering and attract competitive offers from investors and developers and reach commercial and financial close.
Expected Results	The assistance will (i) facilitate the development of a 1-gigawatt solar photovoltaics independent power producer program in Uzbekistan led by ADB, under One ADB approach; (ii) diversify energy sources in Uzbekistan; (iii) decrease the dependence on depleting fossil fuel, gas in particular; (iv) reduce carbon dioxide emissions in energy production generally and for the region of Sherabad in particular; (v) provide positive impact on applicable tariffs in the Uzbekistan energy market; and (vi) increase production of power available for exports, especially to Afghanistan, which is importing 85% of its energy.

---

[11] The Steering Committee of AP3F has approved total 54 projects to date with total fund commitment of $50.6 million. All of these projects have been booked under ADB's Cluster TA 0020-REG. The figure of 1 represents the number of TA approved for AP3F. It does not represent the number of projects AP3F has supported.

2020 Committed Projects and Direct Charges

Projects

ADB Approved Number	Project Name
AP3F043/PP015	PHI: BCDA Public Transportation Public–Private Partnerships (PPP) Project
AP3F044/PP016	PHI: BCDA Information and Communications Technology PPP Project
AP3F045/PD011	AFG: Dahla Dam Hydropower Project
AP3F046/PP017	PHI: O&M for the Metro Manila Subway PPP Project
AP3F047/PP018	PHI: O&M for the North–South Connectivity Railway PPP Project
AP3F048/CB014	MYA: Capacity Building and PPP Certification Program for the Ministry of Transport and Communications
AP3F049/CB015	AZE: PPP Development Center and Project Development Facility
AP3F050/PP019	INO: South Tangerang Waste Management Project
AP3F051/CB016	VIE: Capacity-related Assistance for the Competitive Bidding for Large-Scale Renewable Energy
AP3F052/PD012	PAK: Karachi Waste Water Treatment Project
AP3F053/PP020	UZB: Sherabad Solar Power Phase 2
AP3F054/PM005	TAJ: Project Monitoring Support for the Tajikistan Electric Distribution Company
AP3F055/PM006	TIM: Dili Solid Waste Management Project Monitoring

AFG = Afghanistan, AZE = Azerbaijan, BCDA = Bases Conversion and Development Authority, INO = Indonesia, MYA = Myanmar, O&M = operation and maintenance, OPOH = Office of the Head of the Office of the Public-Private Partnership Department, OPPP = Public-Privae Partnership Department, PAK = Pakistan, PHI = Philippines, TAJ = Tajikistan, TIM = Timor-Leste, UZB = Uzbekistan, VIE = Viet Nam.

Direct Charges

Project Name
1. Hosting and Maintenance of the AP3F Website (2020 services) amounting to $7,757
2. Hosting and Maintenance of the AP3F Website (services until 2021) amounting to $7,557

20 CANADIAN CLIMATE FUND FOR THE PRIVATE SECTOR IN ASIA II (CFPS II)

Donor: Canada

Year Established	2017
Financing Products	Concessional Debt Instruments, Mezzanine, Risk Participation
Objective	Catalyze private sector investment in climate change mitigation and/or adaptation projects in Asia and the Pacific and promote gender equality.
Eligible Sectors	Climate mitigation and adaptation (including infrastructure, agribusiness, financial institutions)
Fund Manager Alternate Fund Manager	Mischa Lentz, Investment Specialist, PSIS Maria Joao Pateguana, Senior Investment Specialist, PSIS

Financial Position as of 31 December 2020
(Amount in $ million)

Cumulative Donor Commitment	Net Balance Available for Trust Fund Committee Allocation		Number of Projects Funded (Approvals)	Number of Projects Funded (Commitments)
Amount	Amount	% of Commitment		
149.46	–	–	7	7

– = Net available balance is commercially sensitive information and cannot be disclosed to the public.

Featured Project

53340-001 - UZB: Navoi Solar Power Project	
Committed Amount	$8.0 million
Commitment Date	December 2020
Expected Completion Date	December 2022
Expected Outcome and/or Purpose	Navoi Solar is the first utility-scale solar project in Uzbekistan. The project entails a 100 megawatt solar power generation facility sited approximately 35 kilometers west of Navoi City. Power will be sold under a 25-year power purchase agreement with Uzbekenergo, the state-owned monopoly power utility.
Expected Results	Concessional loan funded by CFPS II supported the first competitive tender in the country's renewable energy sector and enabled a lower-than-expected power tariff for the project, thereby underscoring the price-competitiveness of the country's solar power sector amid a strong national push toward clean energy.

2020 Committed Projects

ADB Approved Number	Project Name
3801/8370-BAN	Spectra Solar Power
3986/8388-UZB	Navoi Solar Power

BAN = Bangladesh, PSIS = Private Sector Investment Funds and Special Initiatives Division of the Private Sector Operations Department, UZB = Uzbekistan.

21 COOPERATION FUND FOR PROJECT PREPARATION IN THE GREATER MEKONG SUBREGIONAL AND OTHER ASIAN COUNTRIES (AFD GMS)

Donor: France, Agence Française de Développement

Year Established	2004
Financing Products	Technical Assistance (TA)
Objective	The AFD trust fund supports project preparation in the areas of feasibility studies, assessment, prefeasibility, framework of policy preparation for program loan, and transaction advisory services for public-private partnership projects.
Eligible Sectors	Infrastructure and urban planning, health, education and vocational training, agriculture and food security, sustainable development and climate change.
Fund Manager **Alternate Fund Manager**	Jacob Sorensen, Director, SDPF Rajeev Singh, Senior Financing Partnerships Specialist, SDPF

Financial Position as of 31 December 2020
(Amount in $ million)

Cumulative Donor Commitment	Net Balance Available for Trust Fund Committee Allocation		Number of Projects Funded (Approvals)	Number of Projects Funded (Commitments)
Amount	Amount	% of Commitment		
8.51	2.0	24%	15	15

Featured Project

TA 9925-REG: Southeast Asia Transport Project Preparatory Facility Phase 2 (Supplementary)	
Committed Amount	$750,000
Commitment Date	September 2020
Completion Date	December 2022
Expected Outcome and/or Purpose	The TA aims to provide project preparation support and capacity building to the governments of six Southeast Asian developing member countries—Indonesia, Myanmar, the Philippines, Thailand, Timor–Leste, and Viet Nam—for a series of ensuing transport sector projects. The TA has three outputs: (i) feasibility study for ensuing projects prepared, (ii) project implementation activities supported, and (iii) technical and project management capacity of the executing agencies and implementing agencies improved. The trust fund will support the development of the Ha Noi Metro Rail Extension Project (Line No. 3: Ha Noi Railway Station to Hoang Mai Section) in Viet Nam.
Expected Results	The proposed additional financing to the TA facility will assist in achieving the long-term Ha Noi transport master plan objectives by increasing metro coverage and promoting a modal shift from private vehicles to the public transport in Ha Noi, which are consistent with AFD's key focus on mobility and transport. In addition, AFD and ADB have been cofinancing the ongoing Ha Noi Metro Line 3 Project since 2011. Since AFD has experiences of urban railway projects in Asia and South America, the cooperation with AFD through cofinancing will increase a chance of successful project implementation.

2020 Committed Project

ADB Approved Number	Project Name
TA 9925-REG	Southeast Asia Transport Project Preparatory Facility Phase 2 (Supplementary)

REG = regional, SDPF = Partner Funds Division of the Sustainable Development and Climate Change Department.

22 COOPERATION FUND FOR REGIONAL TRADE AND FINANCIAL SECURITY INITIATIVE (RTFSI)

Donors: Australia, Japan, and the United States

Year Established	2004
Financing Products	Investment Project, Technical Assistance (TA)
Objective	RTFSI is a multi-donor umbrella facility that supports ADB TA to developing member countries (DMCs) for enhancing port security (including airports, cargo ports, and containers) and combating money laundering and terrorist financing.
Eligible Sectors	All ADB DMCs and regional institutions within such countries. Priority is afforded to DMCs that are also Asia-Pacific Economic Cooperation economies and are most at risk with regard to money laundering, terrorist financing, or port and airport security.
Fund Manager	Roshan Ouseph, Senior Counsel, OGC

Financial Position as of 31 December 2020
(Amount in $ million)

Cumulative Donor Commitment	Net Balance Available for Trust Fund Committee Allocation		Number of Projects Funded (Approvals)	Number of Projects Funded (Commitments)
Amount	Amount	% of Commitment		
2.78	0.2	7%	9	9

Featured Project

TA 8255-MON: Strengthening the Anti-Money Laundering Regime	
Committed Amount	$720,000
Commitment Date	11 December 2012
Completion Date	31 December 2014 (original); 30 June 2017 (revised)
Outcome and/or Purpose	Government authorities with better capacity to carry out investigation and prosecution of money laundering and terrorism financing offenses
Results	About 40 officers from the participating authorities will be trained in money laundering and terrorism financing trends and typologies, investigation techniques, legal and evidentiary issues, and case preparation for investigation and prosecution. Paper on issues and challenges in the design and implementation of an Anti-Money Laundering and Counter-Financing of Terrorism (AML/CFT) capacity development program using Mongolia as an example.

MON = Mongolia, OGC = Office of the General Counsel.

23 DOMESTIC RESOURCE MOBILIZATION TRUST FUND (DRMTF)

Donor: Japan

Year Established	2017
Financing Products	Technical Assistance (TA), Direct Charge (DC)
Objective	To enhance domestic resource mobilization in ADB's developing member countries and help translate the Sustainable Development Goals into sustaining tax revenues through (i) domestic tax policy and tax administration reform, (ii) regional capacity building programs, and (iii) knowledge products.
Eligible Sectors	Public Sector Management, Multisector
Fund Manager	Daisuke Miura, Public Management Specialist, SDTC-GOV

Financial Position as of 31 December 2020
(Amount in $ million)

Cumulative Donor Commitment	Net Balance Available for Trust Fund Committee Allocation		Number of Projects Funded	Number of Projects Funded
Amount	Amount	% of Commitment	(Approvals)	(Commitments)
7.17	3.19	44%	26 (DC)	26 (DC)

Featured Project

DRMTFDC0017-REG: Development of the Comparative Analysis Series on Tax Administration in Asia and the Pacific (5th Edition)	
Committed Amount	$225,000, financed in full by DRMTF
Commitment Date	January 2020
Expected Completion Date	December 2021
Expected Outcome and/or Purpose	Enhanced knowledge of policymakers and administrators to design effective and efficient tax policies and administrations processes.
Expected Results	The ADB publication, *A Comparative Analysis of Tax Administration in Asia and the Pacific (5th Edition)*, will be released.

2020 Committed Direct Charges

Project Name
REG: Pilot Programs on International Academy for Tax Crime Investigation
REG: Comparative analysis of tax administration in Asia and the Pacific [5th Edition]
REG: A Digital VAT Policy Design and Implementation Toolkit for DMCs
REG: Comprehensive Assessment of Tax Capacity in Southeast Asia
ARM: Tax Policy Review

Project Name
INO: Land Value Capture Policy Development and Implementation
FIJ: Building Systems and Capacity for Compliance Risk Analysis and Management
PHI: Enhancing Philippines tax administration and improving taxpayer service quality through a taxpayer registration database management system
MON: Support for tax data analytics in Mongolia

ARM = Armenia, FIJI = Fiji, INO = Indonesia, MON = Mongolia, PHI = Philippines, REG = regional, SDTC-GOV = Governance Thematic Group of the Sustainable Development and Climate Change Department, VAT = value-added tax.

24 FUTURE CARBON FUND (FCF)

Donors: Finland; Swedish Energy Agency; Participatie Maatschappij Vlaanderen NV for Flemish Region of Belgium; the Republic of Korea; POSCO (Republic of Korea); and Eneco Energy Trade (The Netherlands)

Year Established	2008
Financing Products	Carbon finance through pre-purchase of Certified Emission Reductions (CERs) from eligible Clean Development Mechanism (CDM) projects
Objective	ADB established the Future Carbon Fund (FCF) to enhance the competitiveness of low-carbon technologies and contribute to greenhouse gas (GHG) emission reduction efforts in Asia and the Pacific by providing carbon finance through the pre-purchase of CERs generated by CDM projects in the 2013–2020 period. The FCF also seeks to assist its participants that have mandatory or voluntary GHG reduction targets and policies beyond 2012 by providing ongoing access to CERs.
Eligible Sectors	Multisector (Renewable Energy, Energy Efficiency, Transport, and Waste Management)
Fund Manager	Virender Kumar Duggal, Principal Climate Change Specialist, SDCD

Financial Position as of 31 December 2020
(Amount in $ million)

Cumulative Donor Commitment	Net Balance Available for Trust Fund Committee Allocation		Number of Projects Funded (Approvals)	Number of Projects Funded (Commitments)
Amount	Amount	% of Commitment		
115.00	12.37	11%	33	35

Featured Projects

43936-014 – THA: Solar Power Project	
Approved Amount	$3.23 million
Approval Date	22 July 2011 (signing date–FCF contract)
Completion Date	18 September 2020 (FCF contract)
Outcome and/or Purpose	The project involves the construction and operation of a 55-megawatt AC (net) solar photovoltaic power project located in Lopburi Province in central Thailand, approximately 155 kilometers north of Bangkok. It is the first solar power project to achieve CDM registration in Thailand. The project contributes to reduction of greenhouse gas emissions through exporting renewable power and replacing fossil fuel-based electricity. The project was registered under CDM in September 2011. The project is also delivering variety of co-benefits to the communities including energy access, employment generation, improved livelihoods, and diffusion of low-carbon technologies, among others.
Results	As of 31 December 2020, FCF has disbursed the entire $3.23 million to the project, under three transactions.

SDCD = Climate Change and Disaster Risk Management Division of the Sustainable Development and Climate Change Department, THA = Thailand.

40625-013 – PRC: Lanzhou Sustainable Urban Transport Project	
Approved Amount	$72,835
Approval Date	14 July 2010 (start sate as per eOperations), 7 February 2012 (signing date–FCF contract)
Completion Date	31 December 2018 (end date as per eOperations), Q1 2021 (FCF contract)
Outcome and/or Purpose	The project involves the construction and operation of a Bus Rapid Transit (BRT) system and supporting facilities in Lanzhou City that meets the growing demand for efficient urban transport in the People's Republic of China (PRC). The project consists of (i) 12.3 kilometers of urban roads, including BRT stations and non-motorized transport lanes; (ii) advanced traffic management through real-time monitoring of buses; (iii) advanced environmental monitoring; and (iv) capacity building to support project implementation and BRT operation and management. Through the advance and efficient BRT systems, the project is delivering co-benefits by reducing traffic congestion and upgrading urban transport services to local beneficiaries.

The project contributes to reduction of greenhouse gas emissions and was registered as a CDM project activity in July 2012. |
| Results | As of 31 December 2020, FCF disbursed a total of $72,835 to the project. |

2020 Supported Projects

In 2020, the Fund disbursed $2.22 million worth of carbon finance to 10 projects located in Bangladesh, Fiji, India, Nepal, PRC, and Thailand. Out of the $2.22 million, $0.34 million worth of carbon finance was disbursed to three ADB-funded projects contracted under the FCF.

In 2020, ADB, as the trustee of FCF, did not execute any new CER purchase agreements and made no new commitments to the project developers.

25 HIGH-LEVEL TECHNOLOGY FUND (HLT FUND)

Donor: Japan

Year Established	2017
Financing Products	Investment Project, Technical Assistance (TA), Direct Charge
Objective	To promote integration of high-level technology and innovation solutions in project design and implementation into ADB projects
Eligible Sectors	Priority sectors are Energy, Health, Transport, Urban, and Water but all sectors and themes are eligible to apply.
Fund Manager	Lin Lu, Principal Operations Coordination Specialist, SDOD

Financial Position as of 31 December 2020
(Amount in $ million)

Cumulative Donor Commitment	Net Balance Available for Trust Fund Committee Allocation		Number of Projects Funded (Approvals)	Number of Projects Funded (Commitments)
Amount	Amount	% of Commitment		
70.32	17.81	25%	37	37

Featured Projects

TA 9079-PHI: Strengthening Social Protection Reforms (Supplementary)	
Committed Amount	$1,000,000
Committed Date	10 July 2020
Expected Completion Date	31 December 2023
Expected Outcome and/or Purpose	The education and health profile of the children of program, Pantawid Pamilyang Pilipino Program (4Ps) households are improved.
Expected Results	The advice is timely provided in key policy areas and themes of social protection as identified by the Department of Social Welfare and Development and the national advisory committee for the conditional cash transfer program, 4Ps.

TA 9950-REG: Regional Support to Address the Outbreak of Coronavirus Disease 2019 and Potential Outbreaks of Other Communicable Diseases	
Committed Amount	$300,000
Committed Date	16 November 2020
Expected Completion Date	30 December 2022
Expected Outcome and/or Purpose	The developing member countries' (DMCs) capacities to prevent and contain the COVID-19 outbreak and other communicable diseases are strengthened.
Expected Results	The following are the expected results (i) health outcomes in Asia and the Pacific improved, (ii) access to improved health services increased (Operational Plan 1 of Strategy 2030), and (iii) regional initiatives to reduce cross-border health risks increased.

TA 6563-REG: Regional Support to Build Virus Resilient and Energy Efficient Centralized Air-Conditioning Systems

Committed Amount	$500,000
Committed Date	12 September 2020
Expected Completion Date	31 December 2021
Expected Outcome and/or Purpose	The deployment of centralized air-conditioning systems that meet energy efficiency and indoor air hygiene needs are increased.
Expected Results	The disease resilient clean energy development in DMCs is promoted.

TA 9887-MON: Sustainable Fodder Management (Supplementary)

Committed Amount	$400,000
Committed Date	26 August 2020
Expected Completion Date	30 Nov 2021
Expected Outcome and/or Purpose	The sustainable fodder management practices (production, processing, storage, and supply) are adopted.
Expected Results	The sustainable and economically viable fodder industry in Mongolia is improved.

TA 9984-NAU: Digital Twin Capabilities in Project Management

Committed Amount	$225,000
Committed Date	21 May 2020
Expected Completion Date	31 December 2021
Expected Outcome and/or Purpose	The Government of Nauru's capacity to monitor port project is improved.
Expected Results	Effective project implementation of port project in terms of improved transport infrastructure and reliable and affordable public transport service provided to the Nauru population.

2020 Committed Projects and Direct Charges

Projects

ADB Approved Number	Project Name
TA 9456-ARM	Social Sectors Reform Program (Supplementary)
TA 6570-GEO	Supporting High-Level Technology for Asset Management
TA 9609-INO	Building Inclusive Social Assistance (Supplementary)
TA 9678-INO	Supporting the Advanced Knowledge and Skills for Sustainable Growth Project (Supplementary)
Grant 0684-MON	Community Vegetable Farming for Livelihood Improvement-Additional Financing
Grant 0696-MON	First Utility-Scale Energy Storage
TA 9887-MON	Sustainable Fodder Management (Supplementary)
TA 9984-NAU	Digital Twin Capabilities in Project Management

ADB Approved Number	Project Name
TA 9079-PHI	Strengthening Social Protection Reforms (Supplementary)
TA 6563-REG	Regional Support to Build Virus Resilient and Energy Efficient Centralized Air-Conditioning Systems
TA 6672-REG	Empowering Developing Member Countries to Use Multispectral Satellite Images and Artificial Intelligence for Land Use and Coastal Planning
TA 9170-REG	Promoting Smart Systems in ADB's Future Cities Program (Supplementary)
TA 9420-REG	Implementation of Sustainable Transport for All (Supplementary)
TA 9601-REG	Developing the Health Sector in the Pacific (Supplementary)
TA 9634-REG	Strengthening Integrated Flood Risk Management (Supplementary)
TA 9928-REG	Developing Innovative Community-Based Long-Term Care Systems and Services (Supplementary)
TA 9950-REG	Regional Support to Address the Outbreak of Coronavirus Disease 2019 and Potential Outbreaks of Other Communicable Diseases (Supplementary)
TA 9965-REG	Support for Innovation and Technology Partnerships in Asia and the Pacific – High-Level Technology Application to Address Development Challenges (Subproject 3)

ARM = Armenia, GEO = Georgia, INO = Indonesia, MON = Mongolia, NAU = Nauru, PHI = Philippines, REG = regional, SDOD = Office of the Director General of the Sustainable Development and Climate Change Department.

Direct Charges

Project Name
Support for Innovation and Technology Partnerships in Asia and the Pacific
High-Level Technology Fund Communications Coordinator

26 INTEGRATED DISASTER RISK MANAGEMENT FUND (IDRMF)

Donor: Canada

Year Established	2013
Financing Products	Grant, Technical Assistance (TA), Direct Charge (DC)
Objective	The fund supports activities centered on ADB's integrated disaster risk management framework—combining disaster risk finance, disaster risk reduction, and climate change adaptation to build disaster resilience—developing practical regional integrated disaster risk management (IDRM) measures in line with the disaster risk management priorities of ADB's developing member countries (DMCs) in Southeast Asia.
Eligible Sectors	Multisector
Fund Manager	Preety Bhandari, Chief of Climate Change and Disaster Risk Management Thematic Group concurrently Director, SDCD
Alternate Fund Manager	Steven Goldfinch, Disaster Risk Management Specialist, SDCD

Financial Position as of 31 December 2020
(Amount in $ million)

Cumulative Donor Commitment	Net Balance Available for Trust Fund Committee Allocation		Number of Projects Funded (Approvals)	Number of Projects Funded (Commitments)
Amount	Amount	% of Commitment		
9.74	Fully committed	0%	10	10

Featured Projects

TA 9728-REG: Scoping of Community Resilience Partnership Program	
Committed Amount	$375,000
Commitment Date	23 April 2019
Completion Date	30 September 2020
Outcome and/or Purpose	Undertake a scoping exercise for establishing the Community Resilience Partnership Program (CRPP). Its establishment is in response to the increase in climate and disaster risks, to which more and more communities are being exposed due to rampant and unplanned development in many countries. To manage this, investments in resilience need to reach scale. CRPP aims to support ADB's DMCs scale-up resilience through targeted investments that strengthen resilience of the poor, design and implementation of resilience-building financing mechanism that provide financial resources to the poor and vulnerable communities, and strengthening institutions and processes that provide space to engage the poor and vulnerable in resilience policy- and programs-related decision-making.
Results	The scoping exercise was successfully completed, resulting in the development and launch of the CRPP, including the confirmation of financial resources for the CRPP Financing Partnership Facility. The program will be implemented over the period 2021–2030, and will provide support related to action research, project development, and capacity building for local actions on resilience.

TA 8812-REG: Enhanced Use of Disaster Risk Information for Decision Making in Southeast Asia

Committed Amount	$3,075,000
Committed Date	11 December 2014
Completion Date	30 September 2018
Outcome and/or Purpose	Strengthen the capacity of government officials in Cambodia, the Lao PDR, Myanmar, the Philippines, and Thailand to use disaster risk information for investment planning processes.
Results	**Pipeline development.** The IDRM Fund supported the development of pipeline investment on city government disaster insurance pool for the Philippines. Recognizing many cities in the Philippines face particularly high disaster risk, the pooled insurance arrangement was intended to help address the significant financing gap for rapid post-disaster financing, at the same time reducing the cost of premiums through the pooled arrangement by diversifying risk and absorbing the first layer of loss from pool reserves, in turn reducing the amount of reinsurance required to protect the pool. ADB plans to support the implementation of the pool through a disaster risk financing loan ($100 million) for the Philippines, beginning with a pilot pool arrangement for 10 cities and scaling-up to include additional ones.

TA 8570-REG: Support to Community-Based Disaster Risk Management in Southeast Asia

Committed Amount	$1,750,000
Committed Date	9 December 2013
Completion Date	30 September 2017
Outcome and/or Purpose	Aims to (i) support innovative pilot subprojects on strengthening community disaster resilience, (ii) facilitate peer-to-peer learning among local governments and community-based organizations on disaster resilience, and (iii) provide guidance on scaling-up community-based DRM.
Results	**Innovation.** The IDRM Fund supported the design of a financial scheme for microfinance institutions to support rapid recovery of their clients in the aftermath of disasters (subproject under TA 8570). The scheme proposed a combination of portfolio insurance for microfinance institutions against extreme weather events and an emergency liquidity facility that would be made available in the aftermath of a climate-related disaster. **Pilot activities.** The IDRM Fund supported pilots on community resilience (subprojects under TA 8570). The pilots (i) supported community-based women's organizations to engage with local authorities in accessing resources from local development funds to implement their disaster resilience priorities, (ii) undertook research on cost-and-benefit analysis of community-led resilient infrastructure, and (iii) explored the potential of scaling-up community resilience through investments in social protection and community-driven development. Lessons from the pilots were used to inform the development of (i) ADB's investment in Myanmar Resilient Community Development Project ($198 million), and (ii) the regional TA on Advancing Resilient and Inclusive Development targeted at the Urban Poor ($5 million).

2020 Committed Projects and Direct Charges

Projects

ADB Approved Number	Project Name
TA 9159-REG	Legal Readiness for Climate Finance and Climate Investments (Supplementary)
TA 9728-REG	Scoping of Community Resilience Partnership Program (Supplementary)

Direct Charges

Project Name
IDRMF-DC-0010: Support to the Development of the ASEAN AADMER Work Programme 2021–2025 ($57,500)
IDRMF-DC-0011: Support to the Development of the ASEAN AADMER Work Programme 2021–2025: DRM Specialist ($14,000)

AADMER = ASEAN Agreement on Disaster, Management, and Emergency Response; ASEAN = Association of Southeast Asian Nations; REG = regional; SDCD = Climate Change and Disaster Risk Management Division of the Sustainable Development and Climate Change Department.

27 IRELAND TRUST FUND FOR BUILDING CLIMATE CHANGE AND DISASTER RESILIENCE IN SMALL ISLAND DEVELOPING STATES (BCCDR)

Donor: Government of Ireland, Department of Foreign Affairs and Trade

Year Established	2019
Financing Products	Grant, Technical Assistance (TA), Direct Charge
Objective	To increase small island developing states (SIDS) resilience to disasters caused by natural hazards and to the impact of climate change.
Eligible Sectors	Climate and Disaster Resilience
Fund Manager	Noelle O'Brien, Principal Climate Change Specialist, PAEN

Financial Position as of 31 December 2020
(Amount in $ million)

Cumulative Donor Commitment	Net Balance Available for Trust Fund Committee Allocation		Number of Projects Funded (Approvals)	Number of Projects Funded (Commitments)
Amount	**Amount**	**% of Commitment**		
14.40	–	–	3	3

Featured Project

TA 9963: Strengthening Social Protection in the Pacific	
Committed Amount	$1 million (partly funded by BCCDR)
Commitment Date	24 July 2020
Expected Completion Date	31 March 2025
Expected Outcome and/or Purpose	Strengthen social protection systems and programs in selected Pacific DMCs
Expected Results	(i) Identify and prioritize responsive social protection policies and investments, (ii) build capacity in social protection systems and improve the delivery of social protection services for vulnerable groups, and (iii) strengthen social protection partnerships and produce knowledge products and shared among Pacific developing member countries.

2020 Committed Projects and Direct Charges

Projects

ADB Approved Number	Project Name
TA 9464-REG	Pacific Disaster Resilience Program (Supplementary)
TA 9950-REG	Regional Support to Address the Outbreak of Coronavirus Disease 2019 and Potential Outbreaks of Other Communicable Diseases (Supplementary)
TA 9963-REG	Strengthening Social Protection in the Pacific (Supplementary)

PAEN = Energy Division of the Pacific Department, REG = regional.

Direct Charges

Project Name
Recruitment of Portfolio Management Officer/Fund Administrator

28 JAPAN FUND FOR INFORMATION AND COMMUNICATION TECHNOLOGY (JFICT)

Donor: Japan

Year Established	2001
Financing Products	Grant, Technical Assistance
Objective	To assist developing member countries (DMCs) to bridge the digital divide by supporting information and communication technology (ICT)-related activities that promote poverty reduction, encourage private sector participation in ICT development, and improve regional and international cooperation through ICT applications.
Eligible Sectors	Information and Communication Technology
Fund Manager **Alternate Fund Manager**	Hiroki Kasahara, Principal Financing Partnerships Specialist, SDPF Yusuke Sekiguchi, Financing Partnerships Specialist, SDPF

Financial Position as of 31 December 2020
(Amount in $ million)

Cumulative Donor Commitment	Net Balance Available for Trust Fund Committee Allocation		Number of Projects Funded (Approvals)	Number of Projects Funded (Commitments)
Amount	Amount	% of Commitment		
10.68	0.6	5%	15	15

Featured Projects

Grant 9207-TAJ: Skills and Employability Enhancement Project	
Committed Amount	$1.5 million
Commitment Date	21 October 2020
Expected Completion Date	31 March 2025
Expected Outcome and/or Purpose	The Skills and Employability Enhancement Project aims to promote Tajikistan's inclusive growth by improving the vocational, technical, and soft skills and employability of disadvantaged groups including youth, women, and labor migrants or returning migrants. The outcome will be skills and employability of youth, women, and labor migrants for both domestic and overseas labor market improved.
Expected Results	(i) More inclusive and targeted migration support provided (ii) Access to and relevance of public employment services enhanced (iii) Planning and management of migration and employment services strengthened

2020 Committed Projects

ADB Approved Number	Project Name
Grant 9207-TAJ	Skills and Employability Enhancement

SDPF = Partner Funds Division of the Sustainable Development and Climate Change Department, TAJ = Tajikistan.

29 JAPAN FUND FOR POVERTY REDUCTION (JFPR)

Donor: Japan

Year Established	2000
Financing Products	Grant, Technical Assistance (TA)
Objective	(i) To support innovative poverty reduction and social development activities to help alleviate poverty in developing member countries (DMCs).
	(ii) To help prepare ADB projects or programs; provide sector or economy wide context; project implementation support or policy advice; for institution and capacity-building; knowledge management, and to support regional activities.
Eligible Sectors	All
Fund Manager **Alternate Fund Manager**	Hiroki Kasahara, Principal Financing Partnerships Specialist, SDPF Yusuke Sekiguchi, Financing Partnerships Specialist, SDPF

Financial Position as of 31 December 2020
(Amount in $ million)

Cumulative Donor Commitment	Net Balance Available for Trust Fund Committee Allocation		Number of Projects Funded (Approvals)	Number of Projects Funded (Commitments)
Amount	Amount	% of Commitment		
930.60	131.57	14%	490	487

Featured Projects

Grant 9212-PAL: Disaster Resilient Clean Energy Financing	
Committed Amount	$3 million
Commitment Date	1 December 2020
Expected Completion Date	30 April 2024
Expected Outcome and/or Purpose	The impact is aligned with (i) access to disaster resilient clean energy for consumers increased; (ii) safe, resilient, and prepared communities for calamities and women livelihood recovery enhanced; and (iii) resilience of Palau communities to climate change and disasters enhanced. The outcome will be consumers' energy expenditures reduced.
Expected Results	The Disaster Resilient Clean Energy Financing Project will facilitate access of low-income households and female borrowers to affordable disaster-resilient clean energy financing in Palau through three outputs: (i) disaster-resilient clean energy financing facility for eligible borrowers made available, (ii) accessibility to disaster-resilient clean energy loans for eligible women borrowers improved, and (iii) capacity and awareness of stakeholders increased. The project has strong pro-poor, socially inclusive, and gender-sensitive features. The project will directly benefit approximately 900 households in Palau (or about 3,000 inhabitants), including at least 450 low-income households and 180 households headed by women. They will benefit from reduced households' energy expenditures and improved access to affordable renewable energy.

TA 9913-PHI: Strengthening the Transition of Vulnerable Communities Affected by the Malolos–Clark Railway Project	
Committed Amount	$2 million
Commitment Date	20 May 2020
Expected Completion Date	30 November 2022
Expected Outcome and/or Purpose	Poverty and vulnerability among the Malolos–Clark Railway Project affected persons reduced
Expected Results	(i) To improve financial resilience and stability of at least 1,200 participant households by providing one-on-one mentorship program to effectively engage the participants with Livelihood Restoration and Improvement Program activities, government social support mechanisms, and build capacity in household financial planning and management. (ii) To establish urban resettlement baseline and monitoring system to support project activities, and in the long term, to be used as government's tool for enhanced resettlement monitoring. (iii) To produce knowledge products presenting lessons and best practices in the context of urban resettlement and a framework on how to implement the graduation approach in urban resettlement setting.

2020 Committed Projects and Direct Charges

Projects

ADB Approved Number	Project Name
Grant 9216-CAM	Agricultural Value Chain Competitiveness and Safety Enhancement
Grant 9217-IND	Assam Power Sector Investment Program–Tranche 3
Grant 9210-IND	Delhi-Meerut Regional Rapid Transit System Investment–Tranche 1
Grant 9213-IND	Meghalaya Power Distribution Sector Improvement
Grant 9215-INO	Sustainable Energy Access in Eastern Indonesia—Electricity Grid Development Program (Phase 2)
Grant 9204-MON	Improving Transport Services in *Ger* Areas
Grant 9206-MON	Managing Solid Waste in Secondary Cities
Grant 9208-MON	Support for Inclusive Education
Grant 9202-MON	Ulaanbaatar Community Food Waste Recycling
Grant 9205-MON	Vegetable Production and Irrigated Agriculture
Grant 9212-PAL	Disaster Resilient Clean Energy Financing
Grant 9214-SRI	Small and Medium-Sized Enterprises Line of Credit Project–Third Additional Financing
Grant 9209-TIM	Coffee and Agroforestry Livelihood Improvement
TA 9883-BAN	Support to Quality Enhancement in Primary Education
TA 6537-BHU	Improving Market Linkages for Cottage and Small Industries
TA 6636-IND	Enhancing Community Participation, Gender Mainstreaming, and Institutional Capacity Building of Uttar Pradesh Power Corporation Limited
TA 6658-IND	Strengthening Capacity for Comprehensive Primary Health Care in Urban Areas

ADB Approved Number	Project Name
TA 6635-KAZ	Institutional Support to the National Quality Center for Road Assets
TA 9880-MON	Strengthening Capacity on Disaster Risk Assessment, Reduction and Transfer Instruments in Mongolia
TA 6534-MON	Strengthening Integrated Early Warning System in Mongolia
TA 9913-PHI	Strengthening the Transition of Vulnerable Communities Affected by the Malolos–Clark Railway Project
TA 6609-SRI	Value Chain Development for Tea Sector
TA 9993-THA	Climate Change Adaptation in Agriculture for Enhanced Recovery and Sustainability of Highlands
TA 9955-REG	Building Disaster-Resilient Infrastructure through Enhanced Knowledge
TA 6556-REG	Challenges and Opportunities of Population Aging in Asia: Improving Data and Analysis for Healthy and Productive Aging
TA 6612-REG	COVID-19 Infection Prevention and Control through an Integrated Water, Sanitation, Hygiene, and Health Approach
TA 6539-REG	Investing in Climate Change Adaptation through Agroecological Landscape Restoration: A Nature-Based Solution for Climate Resilience
TA 6594-REG	Mitigating the Impact of COVID-19 through Community-Led Interventions
TA6536-REG	Nowcasting and Disasters: Impact-Based Forecasting and Socioeconomic Monitoring
TA 6669-REG	Promoting Action on Plastic Pollution from Source to Sea in Asia and the Pacific–Prioritizing and Implementing Actions to Reduce Marine Plastic Pollution (Subproject 2)
TA 9681-REG	Southeast Asia Agriculture, Natural Resources, and Rural Development Facility (Supplementary)
TA 9554-REG	Southeast Asia Urban Services Facility (Supplementary)
TA 6671-REG	Technology-Enabled Innovation in Education in Southeast Asia

BAN = Bangladesh, BHU = Bhutan, CAM = Cambodia, COVID-19 = coronavirus disease, IND = India, INO = Indonesia, KAZ = Kazakhstan, MON = Mongolia, PAL = Palau, PHI = Philippines, REG = regional, SDPF = Partner Funds Division of the Sustainable Development and Climate Change Department, SRI = Sri Lanka, THA = Thailand, TIM = Timor-Leste.

Direct Charges

Project Name
Recruitment of Portfolio Management Officer and/or Fund Administrator

30 JAPAN FUND FOR THE JOINT CREDITING MECHANISM (JFJCM)

Donor: Japan

Year Established	2014
Financing Products	Grant, Technical Assistance, Direct Charge
Objective	The fund aims to provide financial incentives for the adoption of advanced low-carbon technologies in ADB-financed and administered sovereign and nonsovereign projects.
Eligible Sectors	Agriculture, Natural Resources, and Rural Development; Energy; Transport; Water and Other Urban Infrastructure and Services; Education; Health; Information and Communication Technology; Multisector; Industry and Trade
Fund Manager	Shintaro Fujii, Environment and Climate Change Specialist, SDCD

Financial Position as of 31 December 2020
(Amount in $ million)

Cumulative Donor Commitment	Net Balance Available for Trust Fund Committee Allocation		Number of Projects Funded (Approvals)	Number of Projects Funded (Commitments)
Amount	**Amount**	**% of Commitment**		
80.43	38.6	48%	7	7

Featured Project

Grant 0733-MLD: Greater Male Waste-to-Energy Project	
Committed Amount	$10 million, grant
Commitment Date	5 February 2020
Expected Completion Date	31 March 2027
Expected Outcome and/or Purpose	Reduce disaster risk and improve climate change resilience while creating a cleaner environment and decreasing greenhouse gas emissions.
Expected Results	The project will establish an integrated regional solid waste management system in Greater Male including collection, transfer, treatment using waste-to-energy (WtE) technology, disposal, recycling, dumpsite closure and remediation, public awareness in reduce-reuse-recycle (3R), and to strengthen institutional capacities for service delivery and environmental monitoring. Specifically, JFJCM will support the development of a 500 tons/day WtE plant, which avoids methane emissions from landfill and replaces diesel-based electricity generation resulting in carbon dioxide emission reductions. The project will not only improve waste management and reduce greenhouse gas emissions, but it will also bring significant environmental, social, and economic benefits, including improvement of marine ecosystem by minimizing wastes dumped to the ocean, improvement of health of the surrounding residents by minimizing the odor and smoke from spontaneous combustion at the landfill, and reduction of diesel oil use resulting in improved energy security and trade balance of Maldives, which heavily depends on imported diesel for power generation.

2020 Committed Projects and Direct Charges

Project

ADB Approved Number	Project Name
Grant 0733-MLD	Greater Male Waste-to-Energy

Direct Charges

Project Name
MLD: Preparation of Knowledge Products on Preparing Outer Islands for Sustainable Energy Development Project (POISED) in Maldives
REG: Survey for Introduction of Hydrogen Infrastructure in Small Island Countries

MLD = Maldives, REG = regional, SDCD = Climate Change and Disaster Risk Management Division of the Sustainable Development and Climate Change Department.

31 JAPAN SCHOLARSHIP PROGRAM (JSP)

Donor: Japan

Year Established	1988
Financing Products	Grant
Objective	To provide opportunities for qualified citizens of ADB's developing member countries to pursue graduate studies in development fields at ADB's partner institutions in Asia and the Pacific.
Eligible Sectors	Education
Fund Manager **Alternate Fund Manager**	Hiroki Kasahara, Principal Financing Partnerships Specialist, SDPF Yusuke Sekiguchi, Financing Partnerships Specialist, SDPF

SDPF = Partner Funds Division of the Sustainable Development and Climate Change Department.

Financial Position as of 31 December 2020
(Amount in $ million)

Cumulative Donor Commitment	Net Balance Available for Trust Fund Committee Allocation		Number of Projects Funded (Approvals)	Number of Projects Funded (Commitments)
Amount	Amount	% of Commitment		
191.57	3.1	2%	–	–

32 LEADING ASIA'S PRIVATE SECTOR INFRASTRUCTURE FUND (LEAP)

Donor: Japan

Year Established	2016
Financing Products	Commercial and Concessional Debt Instruments, Mezzanine Financing, and Equity Investments
Objective	Boost financing for quality, sustainable private infrastructure transactions in Asia and the in Pacific.
Eligible Sectors	Energy (renewable energy generation, energy efficiency and conservation, natural gas transmission and distribution); Transportation; Water and Other Urban Infrastructure and Services
Fund Manager Alternate Fund Manager	Maria Joao Pateguana, Senior Investment Specialist, PSIS Janette Hall, Director, PSIS

Financial Position as of 31 December 2020
(Amount in $ million)

Cumulative Donor Commitment	Net Balance Available for Trust Fund Committee Allocation		Number of Projects Funded (Approvals)	Number of Projects Funded (Commitments)
Amount	Amount	% of Commitment		
1,500.00[12]	–	–	24	23

– = Net available balance is commercially sensitive information and cannot be disclosed to the public.

Featured Projects

JL02-IND: DCDC Health Services Pvt Ltd	
Committed Amount	$5 million
Commitment Date	29 June 2018
Completion Date	Completed and operational
Outcome and/or Purpose	Equity investment was designed to allow DCDC Healthcare Services Private Limited (DCDCPL) expand the reach of its dialysis and ancillary health services in India to more than 180 centers, from the 100 centers in operation at the time of the transaction.
Results	The expansion of the DCDC network improves access to quality dialysis services for end-stage renal diseases especially in under-served and lower-income populations.

---

[12] Cumulative contribution committed refers to total amount pledged of $1.5 billion. These contributions are formally recognized and recorded in ADB's system and financial statements once they are remitted by the financing partner to ADB.

LN8369-REG: Asia Pacific Remote Broadband Internet Satellite Project

Committed Amount	$25 million
Commitment Date	30 November 2019
Completion Date	Completed and operational
Outcome and/or Purpose	Parallel loan for the construction and operation of a shared geostationary, high-throughput satellite bringing broadband internet to remote areas of Asia and the Pacific that are hard to reach with conventional terrestrial internet networks.
Results	The project allows governments of Pacific islands and island nations in the coverage region to connect remote schools and roll out telemedicine programs to remote locations which have limited access to education and medical care

LN8373-VIE: Gulf Solar Power Project

Committed Amount	$7.6 million
Commitment Date	22 January 2020
Expected Completion Date	2021
Expected Outcome and/or Purpose	Concessional loan to construct a 50 megawatt solar power plant and an associated transmission line in the Thanh Thanh Cong Industrial Zone of Tay Ninh Province in southern Viet Nam.
Expected Results	The project is one of Viet Nam's first independent power producers in renewable energy raising an international project finance facility. The project will provide renewable electricity, avoid greenhouse gas emissions, and diversify Viet Nam's fuel mix in line with government priorities.

2020 Committed Projects

ADB Approved Number	Project Name
LN8378-AFG	Afghan Power Plant Company Limited Mazar Gas-Fired Power
LN8381-BAN	Reliance Bangladesh Liquefied Natural Gas and Power–Additional Financing
LN8382-GEO	Georgian Green Bond
LN8379-VIE	B.Grimm Viet Nam Solar Power
LN8386-REG	Indorama Ventures Regional Blue Loan
7643-IND	Avaada Solar Phase 2
7636-REG	Asian Sustainable Infrastructure Mobilization

AFG = Afghanistan, BAN = Bangladesh, GEO = Georgia, IND = India, PSIS = Private Sector Investment Funds and Special Initiatives Division of the Private Sector Operations Department, REG = regional, VIE = Viet Nam.

33 PEOPLE'S REPUBLIC OF CHINA POVERTY REDUCTION AND REGIONAL COOPERATION FUND (PRCF)

Donor: People's Republic of China

Year Established	2005
Financing Products	Grant, Technical Assistance (TA)
Objective	To contribute to poverty reduction, regional cooperation and knowledge sharing, and economic and social development in developing member countries (DMCs) in an accelerated manner and with tangible results.
Eligible Sectors	All ADB sectors, with preference to Energy; Transport; Water and Other Urban Infrastructure and Services; and Agriculture, Natural Resources, and Rural Development
Fund Manager	Guangtao Qi, Financing Partnerships Specialist, SDPF

Financial Position as of 31 December 2020
(Amount in $ million)

Cumulative Donor Commitment	Net Balance Available for Trust Fund Committee Allocation		Number of Projects Funded (Approvals)	Number of Projects Funded (Commitments)
Amount	Amount	% of Commitment		
90.00	24.90	28%	112	112

Featured Projects

TA 9950-REG: Regional Support to Address the Outbreak of Coronavirus Disease 2019 and Potential Outbreaks of Other Communicable Diseases	
Committed Amount	$68.6 million, of which $2.0 million is cofinanced from the Fund
Commitment Date	8 April 2020
Expected Completion Date	28 February 2022
Expected Outcome and/or Purpose	DMCs' capacities to prevent and contain the COVID-19 outbreak and other communicable diseases strengthened.
Expected Results	(i) Support to DMCs affected and potentially affected by the coronavirus disease 2019 and other communicable diseases provided, (ii) economic and health system assessments on the potential effect of the coronavirus disease 2019 conducted, (iii) regional and country-specific health security capabilities strengthened, and (iv) development of sovereign and nonsovereign health security projects to address communicable diseases supported.

TA 6694-REG: Supporting the Central Asia Regional Economic Cooperation Institute	
Committed Amount	$2.0 million, of which $1.0 million is financed from the fund
Commitment Date	18 December 2020
Expected Completion Date	30 September 2023
Expected Outcome and/or Purpose	The CAREC Institute functioning as an independent entity delivering high-quality knowledge services
Expected Results	(i) Institutional capacity and financial sustainability strengthened, (ii) knowledge functions enhanced, and (iii) knowledge management improved.

2020 Committed Projects

ADB Approved Number	Project Name
TA9938-MON	Methane Gas Supply Chain Development Master Plan
TA9839-PAK	Preparing Urban Development Projects (Supplementary)
TA9987-UZB	Road Subsector Development Strategy and Action Plan (Supplementary)
TA6535-REG	Addressing Health Threats in Central Asia Regional Economic Cooperation Countries and the Caucasus
TA6592-REG	Building Financial Resilience and Stability to Reinvigorate Growth
TA9953-REG	Creating Ecosystems for Green Local Currency Bonds for Infrastructure Development in ASEAN+3
TA6699-REG	Enhancing Knowledge as Public Goods for Project Innovation, Demonstration, and Replication
TA9916-REG	Greater Mekong Subregion Sustainable Agriculture and Food Security Program (Supplementary)
TA9950-REG	Regional Support to Address the Outbreak of Coronavirus Disease 2019 and Potential Outbreaks of Other Communicable Diseases (Supplementary)
TA9971-REG	Southeast Asia Agriculture, Natural Resources, and Rural Development Facility–Phase II (Supplementary)
TA6558-REG	Strengthening Knowledge and Capacities for the Design and Implementation of Free Trade Agreements Involving Central Asia Regional Economic Cooperation Countries
TA9963-REG	Strengthening Social Protection in the Pacific
TA6694-REG	Supporting the Central Asia Regional Economic Cooperation Institute

CAREC = Central Asia Regional Economic Cooperation, COVID-19 = coronavirus disease, MON = Mongolia, PAK = Pakistan, REG = regional, SDPF = Partner Funds Division of the Sustainable Development and Climate Change Department, UZB = Uzbekistan.

34 PROJECT READINESS IMPROVEMENT TRUST FUND (PRITF)

Donor: Nordic Development Fund

Year Established	2016
Financing Products	Technical Assistance (TA), Project Design Advance, Multitranche Financing Facility
Objective	The Project Readiness Improvement Trust Fund is a multi-donor financing facility administered by ADB to help countries deliver their respective Nationally Determined Contributions and focus on critical infrastructure investment projects addressing climate change. PRI TF supports upstream preparatory activities, namely, climate risk vulnerability assessments (CRVAs), engineering designs incorporating climate-resilient measures and greater safety factors, feasibility studies and project design reports, bidding documents and procurement plans, knowledge transfer and on-the-job training of central and local partners, and customized climate-resilient solutions. It complements existing ADB project start-up support facilities to enhance project readiness for fast rollout by saving 6 to 24 months in the procurement process, quicker start-up on the ground, and faster fund disbursement.
Eligible Sectors	All developing member countries in Southeast Asia are eligible to access the fund. Assistance to date has been tapped to prepare projects across the agriculture, transport, and tourism sectors, and for strengthening climate resilience of urban services.
Fund Manager **Fund Secretariat Alternate**	Ramesh Subramaniam, Director General, SERD Alely Bernardo, Financing Partnerships Specialist, SERC

Financial Position as of 31 December 2020
(Amount in $ million)

Cumulative Donor Commitment	Net Balance Available for Trust Fund Committee Allocation		Number of Projects Funded (Approvals)	Number of Projects Funded (Commitments)
Amount	**Amount**	**% of Commitment**		
7.80	0.2	0.2%	12	12

Featured Project

TA9323-LAO: Sustainable Rural Infrastructure and Watershed Management Sector Project	
Committed Amount	$ 0.5 million
Commitment Date	17 July 2017
Expected Completion Date	30 April 2022
Expected Outcome and/or Purpose	Sustainable, market-oriented agricultural production, and natural resources management in selected watersheds.
Expected Results	(i) Improved rural incomes from market-driven diversified farm output, watershed health, and community nutrition in the four northern provinces of Houaphan, Louangphabang, Xaignabouli, and Xiangkhouang through (a) promotion of diversification into dry season high-value crops and provision of irrigation and access; (b) protection of watershed ecological services; and (c) improvement of nutrition through awareness building and water, sanitation, and hygiene (WASH) facilities. (ii) Ensured sustainable water resources management with stronger project ownership through capacity building and learning-by-doing.

LAO = Lao People's Democratic Republic, SEOD = Office of the Director General of the Southeast Asia Department, SERC = Regional Cooperation and Operations Coordination Division of the Southeast Asia Department, SERD = Southeast Asia Department.

35 REPUBLIC OF KOREA E-ASIA AND KNOWLEDGE PARTNERSHIP FUND (EAKPF)

Donor: The Republic of Korea

Year Established	2006
Financing Products	Grant, Investment Project, Technical Assistance (TA)
Objective	To contribute to poverty reduction and economic and social development through reducing digital divide and promoting knowledge cooperation between ADB, its developing member countries, and the Republic of Korea.
Eligible Sectors	All Sectors
Fund Manager Alternate Fund Manager	Hyoung Ryoul Lee, Principal Financing Partnerships Specialist, SDPF Seo Hye Shin, Financing Partnerships Specialist, SDPF

Financial Position as of 31 December 2020
(Amount in $ million)

Cumulative Donor Commitment	Net Balance Available for Trust Fund Committee Allocation		Number of Projects Funded (Approvals)	Number of Projects Funded (Commitments)
Amount	Amount	% of Commitment		
122.18	33.6	27%	150	148

Featured Project

TA 9048-REG: Promoting Smart Drinking Water Management in South Asian Cities	
Committed Amount	$1,000,000
Commitment Date	19 October 2015
Completion Date	31 December 2020
Outcome and/or Purpose	The TA aims to improve institutional capacity to respond to increasing needs of operational efficiency and financial sustainability in urban drinking water supply systems.
Results	(i) Operational efficiency improvement plan developed, (ii) knowledge-building and skills development programs on smart drinking water management and technologies implemented, (iii) financial sustainability improvement plans prepared, (iv) new drinking water public–private partnership contract modalities introduced, and (v) study visits and workshops conducted.

2020 Committed Projects and Direct Charges

Projects

ADB Approved Number	Project Name
TA6650-AZE	Fostering Development of Local Tech Startups
TA9980-IND	Strengthening Universal Health Coverage in India: Supporting the Implementation of Pradhan Mantri Jan Arogya Yojana

ADB Approved Number	Project Name
TA6583-INO	Electric Transportation and Charging Infrastructure
TA9946-KAZ	Promoting Digital Technologies for Sustainable Development
TA6564-KAZ	Supporting Renewable Technology-Inclusive Heat Supply Legislation
TA9906-MON	Improving Transport Services in *Ger* Areas
TA9938-MON	Methane Gas Supply Chain Development Master Plan
TA9987-UZB	Road Subsector Development Strategy and Action Plan
TA6592-REG	Building Financial Resilience and Stability to Reinvigorate Growth
TA6672-REG	Empowering Developing Member Countries to Use Multispectral Satellite Images and Artificial Intelligence for Land Use and Coastal Planning
TA9572-REG	Enhancing Effectiveness of Subregional Programs to Advance Regional Cooperation and Integration in Southeast Asia (Supplementary)
TA9621-REG	Green and Innovative Finance Initiative for Scaling Up Southeast Asian Infrastructure (Supplementary)
TA9943-REG	Facilitating Knowledge for Innovation and Technology Cooperation to Accelerate Development
TA9960-REG	Integrated High Impact Innovation in Sustainable Energy Technology: Pilot Testing of Innovative Energy
TA6529-REG	Planning for Economic Recovery of South Asia from COVID-19
TA9968-REG	Preparing Projects to Enhance Transport Connectivity and Resilience in the Pacific (Supplementary)
TA6669-REG	Promoting Action on Plastic Pollution from Source to Sea in Asia and the Pacific–Prioritizing and Implementing Actions to Reduce Marine Plastic Pollution (Subproject 2)
TA6600-REG	Promoting Cross-Border Financial Transactions in the ASEAN+3 Region: Support to the Cross-Border Settlement Infrastructure Forum under the Asian Bond Markets Initiative Medium-Term Road Map, 2019–2022
TA9461-REG	Protecting and Investing in Natural Capital in Asia and the Pacific (Supplementary)
TA6585-REG	Impact Evaluation of Financial Technology Innovations in Selected Developing Member Countries
TA9950-REG	Regional Support to Address the Outbreak of Coronavirus Disease 2019 and Potential Outbreaks of Other Communicable Diseases (Supplementary)
TA6645-REG	Strengthening Resilience and Stability of Banking and Nonbank Financial Systems in Asia
TA9963-REG	Strengthening Social Protection in the Pacific
TA6602-REG	Supporting Startup Ecosystem in the Central Asia Regional Economic Cooperation Region to Mitigate Impact of COVID-19 and Support Economic Revival
TA9967-REG	Using Digital Technology to Improve National Health Insurance in Asia and the Pacific

AZE = Azerbaijan, COVID-19 = coronavirus disease, IND = India, INO = Indonesia, KAZ = Kazakhstan, MON = Mongolia, REG = regional, SDPF = Partner Funds Division of the Sustainable Development and Climate Change Department, UZB = Uzbekistan.

Direct Charges

Project Name
DC00001: Strengthening Operational Support and Communication for EAKPF ($120,000)

36 SPANISH COOPERATION FUND FOR TECHNICAL ASSISTANCE (TAGF-SPA)

Donor: Spain

Year Established	2000
Financing Products	Technical Assistance (TA)
Objective	The fund supports project preparation and transaction advisory services.
Eligible Sectors	Water (and Other Urban Infrastructure Services, including Digital Technology for Development), Energy, Transport, Sustainable, and Smart Cities.
Fund Manager Alternate Fund Manager	Jacob Sorensen, Director, SDPF Rajeev Singh, Senior Financing Partnerships Specialist, SDPF

Financial Position as of 31 December 2020
(Amount in $ million)

Cumulative Donor Commitment	Net Balance Available for Trust Fund Committee Allocation		Number of Projects Funded (Approvals)	Number of Projects Funded (Commitments)
Amount	Amount	% of Commitment		
14.38	4.0	28%	25	25

Featured Project

TA 8135-PHI: Design of a Pilot Project to Improve Environmental Conditions of Estero de Paco	
Committed Amount	$220,000
Commitment Date	8 August 2012
Completion Date	30 April 2015
Outcome and/or Purpose	The expected outcome was a sustainable pilot project designed and implemented for cleaning Pasig River esteros in the Philippines.
Results	See project results in the Technical Assistance Completion Report at https://www.adb.org/projects/documents/design-pilot-project-improve-environmental-conditions-estero-de-paco-tcr

PHI = Philippines, SDPF = Partner Funds Division of the Sustainable Development and Climate Change Department.

37 AUSTRALIAN CLIMATE FINANCE PARTNERSHIP (ACFP)

Donor: Australia

Year Established	2020
Financing Products	Guarantees and Risk Participation, Unhedged Local Currency Financing, Technical Assistance (returnable and non-returnable), and Grant
Objective	The objective of the fund is to contribute to a more stable, secure and prosperous Indo-Pacific to meet the challenges of climate change. To achieve this objective, the fund will support projects that contribute to the following outcomes: (i) reduced project countries' greenhouse gas emission compared to business-as-usual scenario, (ii) project countries becoming more resilient to the impacts of climate change, (iii) national or sectoral reforms improving the enabling environment for climate finance and ease of doing business in participating countries, and (iv) target countries becoming more supportive of gender equality and women's empowerment in fund-targeted sectors.
Eligible Sectors	Climate mitigation and adaptation. Mitigation project types include, but are not limited to renewable energy, sustainable transport, urban infrastructure, energy efficiency, land use and agribusiness, water supply and sanitation/wastewater treatment, solid waste management, and blue carbon mitigation and/or adaptation activities. Adaptation project types include but are not limited to, water supply and management, agriculture and forestry, land use management, natural resource management, resilient infrastructure, marine and coastal ecosystem protection, healthcare, and disaster risk management.
Fund Manager **Alternate Fund Manager**	David Barton, Principal Investment Specialist, PSIS Janette Hall, Director, PSIS

PSIS = Private Sector Investment Funds and Special Initiatives Division of the Private Sector Operations Department.

Financial Position as of 31 December 2020
(Amount in $ million)

Cumulative Donor Commitment	Net Balance Available for Trust Fund Committee Allocation		Number of Projects Funded	Number of Projects Funded
Amount	Amount	% of Commitment	(Approvals)	(Commitments)
106.00	–	–	–	–

– = Net available balance is commercially sensitive information and cannot be disclosed to the public.

38a CLEAN TECHNOLOGY FUND under the CLIMATE INVESTMENT FUND (CIF-CTF)

Donors: Australia, Canada, France, Germany, Japan, Spain, Sweden, the United Kingdom, and the United States

Year Established	2008
Financing Products	Loan, Grant, Technical Assistance (TA)
Objective	The $5.4 billion Clean Technology Fund (CTF) is empowering transformation in developing countries by providing resources to scale-up low-carbon technologies with significant potential for long-term greenhouse gas emissions savings.
Eligible Sectors	Renewable Energy, Energy Efficiency, and Clean Transport
Fund Manager	Preety Bhandari, Chief of Climate Change and Disaster Risk Management Thematic Group concurrently Director, SDCD
Alternate Fund Manager	Christian Ellermann, Senior Climate Change Specialist, SDCD

Financial Position as of 31 December 2020
(Amount in $ million)

Cumulative Donor Commitment	Net Balance Available for Trust Fund Committee Allocation		Number of Projects Funded (Approvals)	Number of Projects Funded (Commitments)
Amount	Amount	% of Commitment		
1,003.57	NA	NA	36	35

Featured Project

562671 REG: ADB Ventures Financing Partnership Facility	
Committed Amount	$20 million
Commitment Date	September 2020 ADB commitment Date: 31 Dec 2020 (for TA 9948: ADB Ventures TA)
Expected Completion Date	NA
Expected Outcome and/or Purpose	The ADB Ventures Facility will support and invest in early-stage companies ($100,000 to $4 million per investment) with technology-enabled solutions that contribute to climate impact in the Asia and the Pacific.
Expected Results	The expected outcome will be the growth of early-stage companies with technology-enabled solutions that contribute to climate impact in the Asia-Pacific (SDG 13). Conservative estimates show the proposed program has the potential to enable investments leading to greenhouse gas reductions of approximately 0.24 million tCO_2e annually, or 4 million prorated tCO_2e over the investment lifetime.

NA = not available, REG = regional, SDCD = Climate Change and Disaster Risk Management Division of the Sustainable Development and Climate Change Department, tCO_2e = metric tons of carbon dioxide equivalent.

2020 Committed Projects

ADB Approved Number	Project Name
Loan 8377	Southern Thailand Wind power and Battery Energy Storage
TA 9948	ADB Ventures Technical Assistance
Loan 8380	Indonesia: Geothermal Power Generation Project
TA 9960[13]	Integrated High Impact Innovation in Sustainable Energy Technology: Pilot Testing of Innovative Energy Technologies and Business Models (Subproject 3)

---

[13] TA 9960 is part of the ADB Ventures Partnership Facility. Reference: Establishment of the ADB Ventures Financing Partnership Facility.

38b STRATEGIC CLIMATE FUND under the CLIMATE INVESTMENT FUND (CIF–SCF)

Donors: Australia, Canada, Denmark, Germany, Japan, the Republic of Korea, the Netherlands, Norway, Spain, Sweden, Switzerland, the United Kingdom, and the United States

Year Established	2008
Financing Products	Loan, Grant, Technical Assistance (TA)
Objective	Serves as an overarching framework to support three targeted programs with dedicated funding to pilot new approaches with potential for scaled-up, transformational action aimed at a specific climate change challenge or sectoral response. Targeted programs under the SCF include the Forest Investment Program (FIP), the Pilot Program for Climate Resilience (PPCR), and the Program for Scaling-Up Renewable Energy in Low-Income Countries (SREP).
Eligible Sectors	Forest and Land Use Management, Climate Resilience, and Renewable Energy Access
Fund Manager	Preety Bhandari, Chief of Climate Change and Disaster Risk Management Thematic Group concurrently Director, SDCD
Alternate Fund Manager	Christian Ellermann, Senior Climate Change Specialist, SDCD

Financial Position as of 31 December 2020
(Amount in $ million)

Cumulative Donor Commitment	Net Balance Available for Trust Fund Committee Allocation		Number of Projects Funded	Number of Projects Funded
Amount	Amount	% of Commitment	(Approvals)	(Commitments)
441.44	NA	NA	61	61

Featured Project

TA 6629-REG: Improved Decision-making for Climate-Resilient Development in Asia and the Pacific	
Committed Amount	$2.15 million
Commitment Date	30 October 2020
Expected Completion Date	31 March 2023
Expected Outcome and/or Purpose	Decision-making for climate-resilient development in selected DMCs improved.
Expected Results	**Output 1: Country systems for climate risk-informed fiscal decision-making strengthened.** Support provided through proposed diagnostic work, improved understanding of long-term climate risk and opportunities in specific sectors, capacity building on use of climate risk-informed fiscal planning tools and guidelines, and strengthened coordination between ministries and with stakeholders, will lead to improved decision-making for climate-resilient development and development and strengthening of fiscal policy and management processes to support such decision-making.

TA 6629-REG: Improved Decision-making for Climate-Resilient Development in Asia and the Pacific

Output 2: Knowledge on climate risk-informed decision-making enhanced.
The TA is innovative, as it attempts to shift the entry point for climate adaptation from a project level to upstream fiscal and sector planning. Such an approach will allow for the identification of wider processes that can help influence the future pipeline of investments in climate adaptation, including investments that could be potentially be financed by ADB. Furthermore, by promoting a whole-of-society approach toward resilience, the TA aims to systematically engage the private sector in climate adaptation-related investments, which is critical in recognizing the scale of finance needed for climate adaptation.

2020 Committed Projects

ADB Approved Number	Project Name
Grant 0736	Cambodia Grid Reinforcement Project
Grant 0764	Kiribati South Tarawa Renewable Energy Project
TA 9959	BDRP: Strengthening Climate Resilience of Women Engaged in Poultry
TA 6629	BDRP: Improved Decision-Making for Climate-Resilient Development in Asia and the Pacific

BDRP = Business Development for Resilience Program, NA = not available, REG = regional, SDCD = Climate Change and Disaster Risk Management Division of the Sustainable Development and Climate Change Department.

39 GLOBAL AGRICULTURE AND FOOD SECURITY PROGRAM (GAFSP)

Donors: World Bank is the GAFSP Trustee with donors to include Australia, Bill & Melinda Gates Foundation, Canada, Germany, Ireland, Japan, the Republic of Korea, the Netherlands, Norway, Spain, the United Kingdom, and the United States

Year Established	May 2011 (through a Board paper)
Financing Products	Technical Assistance, Grant (blended financing tools are planned to support private sector investments under a revised fund structure to be launched in 2021)
Objective	To improve the income and food security of poor people in developing countries[14] through more public and private investments in the agriculture and rural sectors (Sustainable Development Goal 2).
Eligible Sectors	Agriculture, Natural Resources, and Rural Development
Facility Manager	Michiko Katagami, Principal Natural Resources and Agriculture Specialist, SDTC-AR

Financial Position as of 31 December 2020
(Amount in $ million)

Cumulative Donor Commitment	Net Balance Available for Trust Fund Committee Allocation		Number of Projects Funded (Approvals)	Number of Projects Funded (Commitments)
Amount	Amount	% of Commitment		
67.49	NA	NA	4[15]	4

Featured Projects

Grant 0302-CAM: Emergency Food Assistance Project	
Committed Amount	$24.5 million (fully financed by GAFSP)
Commitment Date	11 September 2012
Actual Closing Date	16 November 2016
Outcome and/or Purpose	To reduce the vulnerability of food-insecure households in the target provinces through improved access to sufficient and nutritious food and production inputs
Results	The project improved the food security of over 55,000 households. Among the beneficiary households, prevalence of severe (from 12% to 4%) and moderately (from 56% to 32%) severe food-insecure households was reduced, while little or no food-insecure households increased from 32% to 64%. Other outcomes include the establishment of food security and nutrition monitoring and evaluation system with MIS and quarterly bulletins, increase of rice yields from 2 t/ha to 3.4 t/ha during dry season and 1.5 t/ha to 2 t/ha during wet season, and improved access to toilets (from 15% to 56%) and increased practice of hand washing (46% increase).

---

14   Countries which are part of the World Bank's International Development Association. https://ida.worldbank.org/.
15   Number of projects approved by ADB (3 Grants, 1 TA). Two additional projects were approved by the Trust Fund Committee in 2020 for ADB processing (i) Additional financing of $3.8 million grant for CAM: Climate-Resilient Rice Commercialization Sector Development Program scheduled in 2021; and (ii) $15 million grant for AFG: Community-Driven Irrigation Management Sector Project ($3 million TA for Food and Agriculture Organization of the United Nations and $12 million grant for the ADB project) scheduled in 2022.

Grant 0349-CAM: Climate-Resilient Rice Commercialization Sector Development Program

Committed Amount	$14.6 million
Commitment Date	27 June 2013
Expected Closing Date	30 September 2021
Expected Outcome and/or Purpose	To enhance the production of quality rice in Cambodia while preserving the natural resource base
Expected Results	The project completed 11 of 12 policy conditions to facilitate climate-resilient rice commercialization. Community-agroecosystem analysis were completed for 100% of the target communities. Land use, soil classification, and rice ecosystem maps were produced for the 13 target districts, while 8 training programs and 3 workshops were organized on land use mapping for 386 participants (8% women). The project rehabilitated irrigation subprojects providing water access to 49,520 farmers (51% women); completed 146 laser land levelling training to 4,740 farmers (40% women); and organized 153 training for 6,786 agricultural cooperative members (36% women). Technical information packages were produced on rice production during dry and wet seasons, rice seed production, pest and diseases, laser land levelling, rice post-harvest technology and agro-eco analysis. Business matching was completed by 767 representatives (24% women) to facilitate linkages with rice millers, agricultural cooperatives, and exporters. The feasibility study of weather indexed crop insurance was completed for pilot testing in May 2020.

Grant 0617-MYA: Climate-Friendly Agribusiness Value Chains Project

Committed Amount	$22 million
Commitment Date	9 October 2018
Expected Closing Date	30 June 2026
Expected Outcome and/or Purpose	To develop productive and resource-efficient agribusiness value chains in the project areas
Expected Results	Recruitment of project implementation consulting firm (PIC) and individual consultants on financial management, procurement, and agriculture digital finance was completed. Procurement of some civil works packages for farm roads and several goods packages have also been completed, while procurement of the rest of the goods, works, and consulting services packages are underway. The contract for the project implementation consultants (PIC) was signed in May 2020. Only national consultants of PIC could be mobilized in August 2020 because of travel restrictions on international consultants imposed due to the coronavirus disease 2019 (COVID-19) pandemic.
	Under output (i), three contracts for a few farm roads worth $0.43 million were awarded in July 2020. Under output (ii), the Department of Agriculture, with support from PIC, is finalizing the terms of reference to recruit the International Rice Research Institute through single source selection. Under output (iii), the Department of Planning has begun to conduct training workshops on monitoring and evaluation to staff at regional and township levels. The inception mission successfully concluded in December 2020.

TA 9694-MYA: Climate-Friendly Agribusiness Value Chains Sector Project	
Committed Amount	$994,937
Commitment Date	17 December 2018
Expected Closing Date	30 June 2026
Expected Outcome and/or Purpose	To support a randomized controlled trial impact evaluation of Grant 0617-MYA: Climate-Friendly Agribusiness Value Chains Project through four interventions: irrigation, advisory services, finance, and nutrition.
Expected Results	Competitive firm selection was completed in 2020, and a contract with IDinsight was issued. Study progress has been impeded by travel restrictions imposed for COVID-19 control.

AFG = Afghanistan, CAM = Cambodia, COVID-19 = coronavirus disease, MYA = Myanmar, SDTC-AR = Rural Development and Food Security (Agriculture) Thematic Group of the Sustainable Development and Climate Change Department, t/ha = tons per hectare.

40 GLOBAL ENVIRONMENT FACILITY (GEF)

Donor: Global Environment Facility (GEF)

Year Established	1991
Financing Products	Technical Assistance (TA), Grant, Non-Grant Instrument
Objective	Provide grants for projects that benefit the global environment (i.e., biodiversity, climate change, international waters, land degradation, sustainable forest management, and chemicals management).
Eligible Sectors	Environmental Sustainability
Facility Manager	Bruce Dunn, Director, SDSS

Financial Position as of 31 December 2020
(Amount in $ million)

Cumulative Donor Commitment	Net Balance Available for Trust Fund Committee Allocation		Number of Projects Funded (Approvals)	Number of Projects Funded (Commitments)
Amount	Amount	% of Commitment		
245.77	NA	NA	76[16]	76

Note: Amounts reflected are projects that were approved and committed by ADB.

Featured Project

49453-002-KIR: South Tarawa Renewable Energy Project	
Committed Amount	$4,457,156
Commitment Date	11 December 2020*
Expected Completion Date	31 December 2027
Expected Outcome and/or Purpose	The Asian Development Bank provided a grant to the Government of Kiribati. The project will combat factors that result in the high incidence of waterborne disease in South Tarawa, the capital of Kiribati, through the delivery and effective management of new and rehabilitated climate-resilient water supply assets and of improved hygiene practices. The Global Environment Fund (GEF) additional financing will progressively introduce climate-resilient asset management into the embryonic national asset management process. This will create a strong foundation for upscaling and rolling out climate-resilient asset management nationally and integrating climate change resilient at key stages.
Expected Results	The GEF component will (i) establish a common data and information platform to provide management and decision-making support to multiple stakeholders, and (ii) proposing strategic use of asset management as a tool to achieve climate resilience.

*GEF commitment date.

---

[16] Number of projects include CEO-endorsed by GEF. Approved and committed number of projects by ADB is 89 for both grants and TA projects.

2020 Committed Project

ADB Approved Number	Project Name
TA9911-REG	Promoting Action on Plastic Pollution from Source to Sea in Asia and the Pacific–Enhancing Knowledge and Creating Enabling Environments for Reducing Marine Plastic Pollution (Subproject 1) (Supplementary)

KIR = Kiribati, REG = regional, SDSS = Safeguards Division of the Sustainable Development and Climate Change Department.

41 GLOBAL PARTNERSHIP FOR EDUCATION FUND (GPE)

Donors: Australia, Belgium, Canada, the Children's Investment Fund Foundation (CIFF), Denmark, the European Commission, Finland, France, Germany, Ireland, Italy, Japan, Luxembourg, the Netherlands, Norway, the Republic of Korea, Romania, the Russian Federation, Senegal, Spain, Sweden, Switzerland, the United Arab Emirates, the United Kingdom, the United States, the Open Society Foundation, Dubai Cares, Stichting Benevolentia (Porticus), and the Rockefeller Foundation

Year Established	2011
Financing Products	Program Development Grant
Objective	GPE mobilizes global and national investments and brings partners together to help governments build strong education systems, based on data and evidence. It brings together developing countries, donors, international organizations, civil society, including youth and teacher organizations, the private sector, and private foundations to pursue the shared objective of equitable, quality education for all.
Eligible Sectors	Focus areas are on the following: (i) gender equality, (ii) education in crisis, (iii) inclusive education, (iv) early education, (v) learning assessments, (vi) teaching quality, and (vii) data systems.
Facility Manager	

Financial Position as of 31 December 2020
(Amount in $ million)

Cumulative Donor Commitment	Net Balance Available for Trust Fund Committee Allocation		Number of Projects Funded (Approvals)	Number of Projects Funded (Commitments)
Amount	Amount	% of Commitment		
1.42	NA	NA	5	5

Featured Project

TA 9645-REG: Strengthening Education in the Pacific Region	
Committed Amount	$389,875
Commitment Date	10 February 2020
Expected Completion Date	30 June 2025
Expected Outcome and/or Purpose	Regional capacity to improve education outcomes in the Pacific enhanced. The purpose of the Program Development Grant is to effectively develop and prepare a program that will support the development of the region's education sector plan which meets the criteria to be financed by the GPE through an Education Sector Program Implementation Grant (ESPIG) and/or a Multiplier Grant.
Expected Results	A program for implementation of the Pacific Regional Education Framework (PACREF) developed. The activities are: (i) strengthening the PACREF Program Facilitating Unit (PFU), (ii) in-country consultations, (iii) strengthening PACREF Program governance, (iv) preparation and finalization of the Pacific Region's ESPIG, (v) all country Review of the Final Pacific Region ESPIG Application Package, and (vi) grant administration training.

2020 Committed Projects

ADB Approved Number	Project Name
TA 9645-REG	Strengthening Education in the Pacific Region (Supplementary)

NA = not available, REG = regional.

42 GREEN CLIMATE FUND (GCF)

Donors: Green Climate Fund, which has received contributions from Austria, Belgium, Brussels Capital Region (Belgium), Bulgaria, Canada, Denmark, Finland, France, Germany, Hungary, Iceland, Indonesia, Ireland, Italy, Japan, Liechtenstein, Luxembourg, Malta, Monaco, the Netherlands, New Zealand, Norway, Poland, Portugal, the Republic of Korea, the Slovak Republic, the Russian Federation, Slovakia, Slovenia, Spain, Sweden, Switzerland, the United Kingdom, and Wallonia (Belgium) https://www.greenclimate.fund/about/resource-mobilisation

Year Established	2010
Financing Products	Grant, Loan, Equity, Guarantee
Objective	The Green Climate Fund (GCF) is a global fund created to support the efforts of developing countries to respond to the challenge of climate change. GCF helps developing countries limit or reduce their greenhouse gas (GHG) emissions and adapt to climate change. It seeks to promote a paradigm shift to low-emission and climate-resilient development, taking into account the needs of nations that are particularly vulnerable to climate change impacts.
Eligible Sectors	Ecosystem; Livelihoods; Transport; Infrastructure Resilience; Forestry and Land Use; Energy access and generation; Health, food and water security; Energy Efficiency
Fund Manager	Preety Bhandari, Chief of Climate Change and Disaster Risk Management Thematic Group concurrently Director, SDCD
Alternate Fund Manager	Christian Ellermann, Senior Climate Change Specialist, SDCD

Financial Position as of 31 December 2020
(Amount in $ million)

Cumulative Donor Commitment	Net Balance Available for Trust Fund Committee Allocation		Number of Projects Funded (Approvals)	Number of Projects Funded (Commitments)
Amount	Amount	% of Commitment		
374.70	NA	NA	10[17]	9

Featured Project

Grant 0653-KIR: South Tarawa Water Supply Project	
Committed Amount	$ 28.6 million (grant)
Commitment Date	October 2018
Expected Completion Date	4 April 2028
Expected Outcome and/or Purpose	The estimated $62 million project will address both adaptation and mitigation objectives by building a 6,000 cubic-meter-per-day (cbm/day) reverse osmosis seawater desalination plant, to provide South Tarawa with a reliable, climate-resilient source of fresh water. The project will also renovate and expand the reticulated water network to reduce leakages and ensure access to the new clean-water source.

---

[17] Number of projects approved by ADB is 11 while number of projects committed is 10. Projects for REG 9425 and COO 3193/0415/0493/0548 are counted as separate projects by ADB.

Grant 0653-KIR: South Tarawa Water Supply Project

	A photovoltaic power plant will also be constructed to offset the greenhouse gas emissions from the desalination plant and the increased water treatment and distribution. The entire population of Tarawa—currently about 53% of Kiribati's population—will benefit directly from the project. Without it, there will be more water shortages as the population grows, and there will be less water of consistently good quality for the most vulnerable people and communities. Carbon dioxide emissions are expected to decrease by 111,323 metric tons over the 20-year period as water pumping is reduced and the country moves away from diesel generation.
Expected Results	62,298 beneficiaries; 89,400 tCO$_2$e reduced per year; 2.5 megawatts of solar photovoltaic installed At least 95% of South Tarawa's population (51.5% of them women) has access to safe, climate-resilient water supplies 6,000 cbm/day desalination capacity is installed

2020 Committed Projects

ADB Approved Number	Project Name
0625/0653	KIR: South Tarawa Water Supply
3799/8366/8367/8368/0649	PAK: Karachi Bus Rapid Transit Red Line

KIR = Kiribati, NA = not available, PAK = Pakistan, SDCD = Climate Change and Disaster Risk Management Division of the Sustainable Development and Climate Change Department, tCO$_2$e = metric tons of carbon dioxide equivalent.

43 WOMEN ENTREPRENEURS FINANCE INITIATIVE (We-Fi)

Donors: Women Entrepreneurs Finance Initiative, Trust Fund managed by the World Bank

Year Established	2017
Financing Products	Technical Assistance (TA), Grant
Objective	To (i) support women-owned or led small and medium-sized enterprises (WSMEs) across developing countries by providing them with access to finance, capacity building, networks and mentors, and opportunities to link with domestic and global markets; and (ii) work with governments and other institutional players to improve the business environment for these enterprises.
Eligible Sectors	Multisector–Finance
Fund Manager Alternate Fund Manager	Samantha Hung, Chief of Gender Equality Thematic Group, SDTC-GEN Keiko Nowacka, Senior Social Development Specialist (Gender and Development), SDTC-GEN

Financial Position as of 31 December 2020
(Amount in $ million)

Cumulative Donor Commitment	Net Balance Available for Trust Fund Committee Allocation		Number of Projects Funded	Number of Projects Funded
Amount	**Amount**	**% of Commitment**	**(Approvals)**	**(Commitments)**
31.11	NA	NA	6	6

Featured Project

Women Accelerating Vibrant Enterprises in Southeast Asia and the Pacific (WAVES) Program	
Committed Amount	$20.2 million, of which $13.37 million for Viet Nam, $5.5 million for Pacific
Commitment Date	September 2019
Expected Completion Date	December 2025
Expected Outcome and/or Purpose	The WAVES Program aims to build capacity across the entrepreneurial ecosystem, in partnership with governments, the private sector and women's businesses, to open new doors and create an empowering environment for women-owned or led small and medium-sized enterprises (WSMEs) to grow and scale-up. The WAVES Program will target 5,105 growth-oriented women's businesses to enable them to become thriving SMEs.
Expected Results	By 2024, the WAVES Program will have (i) strengthened institutional capacity and interest of financial institution partners to actively develop WSME-tailored products, services, and approaches; (ii) positioned WSMEs firmly on the policy agendas of governments, and ensured WSMEs' voices are included in decision-making processes; and (iii) built up WSME's capacity and confidence to run successful businesses, and to increase their contributions to building inclusive and dynamic economies.

Women Accelerating Vibrant Enterprises in Southeast Asia and the Pacific (WAVES) Program

Status as of December 2020

WAVES Program in Viet Nam

In December 2020, ADB Management approved a COVID-19 response project using We-Fi funds which will support at least 500 women-owned/led small and medium-sized enterprises (WSMEs) in Viet Nam to overcome the COVID-19 pandemic. Principal activities include restructuring of loans and loan holidays, complemented by a specialized business counseling program to enable these entrepreneurs to receive dedicated one-on-one business counseling. The counselling program is set to begin in Q1 2021.

WAVES Program in the Pacific

ADB approved in December 2020 two subprojects under the TA cluster REG: Technical Assistance for the Women's Financing Marketplace with the overall outcome of increasing sustainable financial inclusion for women and women's businesses. Subproject 2 will support the identification and design of innovative technologies and suitable and sustainable digital service delivery models to support gender-responsive ecosystems. Subproject 3 will build the capacities of women's businesses and financial institutions.

2020 Committed Projects

ADB Approved Number	Project Name
TA 6646	REG: Women's Financing Marketplace–Innovation and Technology (Subproject 2)
TA 6705	REG: Women's Financing Marketplace–Capacity building (Subproject 3)
Grant 0781	VIE: COVID-19 Relief for Women-led Small and Medium-Sized Enterprises Project

COVID-19 = coronavirus disease, NA = not available, REG = regional, SDTC-GEN = Gender Equality Thematic Group of the Sustainable Development and Climate Change Department, VIE = Viet Nam.

44a ASIA PACIFIC DISASTER RESPONSE FUND (APDRF)

Donors: ADB

Year Established	2009
Financing Products	Grant
Objective	The fund responds to the urgent need for financial assistance immediately after the occurrence of a disaster, providing incremental and quick-disbursing grant resources to any ADB developing member country (DMC) for the restoration of life-preserving services to the affected communities.
Eligible Sectors	Multisector
Fund Manager	Preety Bhandari, Chief of Climate Change and Disaster Risk Management Thematic Group concurrently Director, SDCD
Alternate Fund Manager	Charlotte Benson, Principal Disaster Risk Management Specialist, SDCD

Financial Position as of 31 December 2020
(Amount in $ million)

Cumulative Donor Commitment	Net Balance Available for Trust Fund Committee Allocation		Number of Projects Funded (Approvals)	Number of Projects Funded (Commitments)
Amount	Amount	% of Commitment		
90.00	14.2	15.8%	48	47

Project Highlights

APDRF is an important source of immediate liquidity to ADB DMCs impacted by disasters.

As of 31 December 2020, 47 grants totaling $76.2 million have been committed in response to disasters in 22 countries:

(i)   tropical storms/cyclones in Fiji, Palau, the Philippines, Samoa, Tonga, Vanuatu, and Viet Nam;
(ii) floods in Cambodia, Fiji, Myanmar, Pakistan, Solomon Islands, Sri Lanka, and Thailand;
(iii) droughts in the Marshall Islands and Viet Nam;
(iv) *dzud* in Mongolia;
(v)   earthquakes and tsunamis in Indonesia, Nepal, Papua New Guinea, and Samoa;
(vi) volcanic activity in Vanuatu; and, most recently,
(vii) the COVID-19 pandemic in the Federated States of Micronesia, Indonesia, Maldives, the Marshall Islands, Mongolia, Nauru, Pakistan, Philippines, Tonga, and Tuvalu.

Proceeds have been used for a wide variety of purposes, including the provision of clean water, food, tents, blankets, and medical supplies and equipment; relief logistics and transportation; restoration of community infrastructure and public services; and livelihood restoration, including cash-for-work programs.

2020 Committed Projects

ADB Approved Number	Project Name
Grant 0685	PHI: COVID-19 Emergency Response
Grant 0686	INO: COVID-19 Emergency Response
Grant 0687	MLD: COVID-19 Emergency Response
Grant 0688	MON: COVID-19 Emergency Response
Grant 0689	NAU: COVID-19 Emergency Response
Grant 0690	TUV: COVID-19 Emergency Response
Grant 0691	FSM: COVID-19 Emergency Response
Grant 0692	RMI: COVID-19 Emergency Response
Grant 0693	TON: COVID-19 Emergency Response
Grant 0694	PAK: COVID-19 Emergency Response
Grant 0695	VAN: Tropical Cyclone Harold Emergency Response Project
Grant 0697	FIJ: Tropical Cyclone Harold Emergency Response Project
Grant 0698	TON: Tropical Cyclone Harold Emergency Response Project
Grant 0750	VIE: Viet Nam Tropical Storms Response

COVID-19 = coronavirus disease, FSM = Federated States of Micronesia, INO = Indonesia, MLD = Maldives, MON = Mongolia, NAU = Nauru, PAK = Pakistan, PHI = Philippines, RMI = Marshall Islands, SDCD = Climate Change and Disaster Risk Management Division of the Sustainable Development and Climate Change Department, TON = Tonga, TUV = Tuvalu, VIE = Viet Nam.

44b APDRF GOVERNMENT OF JAPAN FOR COVID-19 (APDRF JPN)

Donor: Japan

Year Established	2020
Financing Products	Grant
Objective	The Government of Japan's contribution to the Asia Pacific Disaster Response Fund (APDRF) responds to the urgent need for financial assistance of ADB's developing member countries, providing quick-disbursing grants of up to $3 million to help strengthen their capacity to contain the spread of the coronavirus disease 2019 (COVID-19).
Eligible Sectors	Multisector
Fund Manager	Preety Bhandari, Chief of Climate Change and Disaster Risk Management Thematic Group concurrently Director, SDCD
Alternate Fund Manager	Charlotte Benson, Principal Disaster Risk Management Specialist, SDCD

Financial Position as of 31 December 2020
(Amount in $ million)

Cumulative Donor Commitment	Net Balance Available for Trust Fund Committee Allocation		Number of Projects Funded (Approvals)	Number of Projects Funded (Commitments)
Amount	Amount	% of Commitment		
75.00	27.1	36.1%	26	25

Featured Project

Grant 0707-TIMOR-LESTE: COVID-19 Food Security Emergency Response	
Committed Amount	$1,000,000
Commitment Date	9 July 2020
Expected Completion Date	28 February 2021
Expected Results	The grant enabled urgent food assistance to be provided to approximately 28,000 food-insecure people—including over 12,000 children and 4,000 older people—across 5 municipalities and 100 villages. The nutritionally balanced food baskets, which included fresh vegetables, fruits, rice, beans, and super foods such as moringa noodles, were sourced from the local market. This farm-to-table emergency food distribution is an innovative approach that has also helped over 1,000 local farmers, and micro and small enterprises who have not been able to sell their products due to COVID-19 emergency restrictions imposed to contain the spread of the virus. The grant contributed to ensuring food and nutrition security for the most vulnerable households. In particular, the grant helped prevent further wasting and stunting in children under 5 years.

2020 Committed Projects

ADB Approved Number	Project Name
Grant 0702	SRI: COVID-19 Emergency Response
Grant 0707	TIM: COVID-19 Food Security Emergency Response
Grant 0712	NEP: COVID-19 Emergency Response
Grant 0715	BHU: COVID-19 Emergency Response
Grant 0716	MLD: COVID-19 Emergency Response
Grant 0719	PNG: COVID-19 Emergency Response
Grant 0720	VAN: COVID-19 Emergency Response
Grant 0721	SAM: COVID-19 Emergency Response
Grant 0722	FSM: COVID-19 Emergency Response
Grant 0723	KIR: COVID-19 Emergency Response
Grant 0724	SOL: COVID-19 Emergency Response
Grant 0725	COO: COVID-19 Emergency Response
Grant 0726	TUV: COVID-19 Emergency Response
Grant 0727	PAL: COVID-19 Emergency Response
Grant 0728	RMI: COVID-19 Emergency Response
Grant 0729	ARM: COVID-19 Emergency Response
Grant 0730	TAJ: COVID-19 Emergency Response
Grant 0731	BAN: COVID-19 Emergency Response Project
Grant 0734	MON: COVID-19 Emergency Response – Phase 2
Grant 0735	KAZ: COVID-19 Emergency Response
Grant 0738	UZB: COVID-19 Emergency Response
Grant 0743	NIU: COVID-19 Emergency Response
Grant 0744	FIJ: COVID-19 Emergency Response
Grant 0745	NAU: COVID-19 Emergency Response
Grant 0773	GEO: COVID-19 Emergency Response Project

ARM = Armenia, BAN = Bangladesh, BHU = Bhutan, COO = Cook Islands, COVID-19 = coronavirus disease, FIJ = Fiji, FSM = Federated States of Micronesia, GEO = Georgia, KAZ = Kazakhstan, KIR = Kiribati, MAL = Maldives, MON = Mongolia, NAU = Nauru, NEP = Nepal, NIU = Niue, PAL = Palau, PNG = Papua New Guinea, RMI = Marshall Islands, SAM = Samoa, SDCD = Climate Change and Disaster Risk Management Division of the Sustainable Development and Climate Change Department, SOL = Solomon Islands, SRI = Sri Lanka, TAJ = Tajikistan, TIM = Timor-Leste, TUV = Tuvalu, UZB = Uzbekistan.

45 CLIMATE CHANGE FUND (CCF)

Donor: ADB

Year Established	2008
Financing Products	Grant Component of Investment, Technical Assistance (TA) (stand-alone and linked to loan), and Direct Charge
Objective	To facilitate greater investments in developing member countries (DMCs) to effectively address the causes and consequences of climate change, by strengthening support to low-carbon and climate-resilient development in DMCs. CCF plays a key role in mainstreaming climate actions in ADB's operations and is critical for achieving the climate targets under Strategy 2030's third operational priority of tackling climate change, building climate and disaster resilience, and enhancing environmental sustainability. The fund focuses on three areas: (i) adaptation; (ii) clean energy development; and (iii) reduced emission from deforestation and degradation and improved land use management.
Eligible Sectors	Multiple
Fund Manager	Preety Bhandari (overall fund manager; coordinator–adaptation and land use), Chief of Climate Change and Disaster Risk Management Thematic Group concurrently Director, SDCD
Fund Coordinator	Robert Guild (coordinator–clean energy), Chief Sector Officer, SDSC

Financial Position as of 31 December 2020
(Amount in $ million)

Cumulative Donor Commitment	Net Balance Available for Trust Fund Committee Allocation		Number of Projects Funded (Approvals)	Number of Projects Funded (Commitments)
Amount	Amount	% of Commitment		
98.00	21.4[18]	22%	124[19]	124

Source: As of 31 December 2020, CCF monitoring database.

Featured Projects

TA 9323-LAO Flood and Drought Mitigation and Management Project	
Committed Amount	Climate Change Fund - $1,300,000
Commitment Date	December 2020 (increase in TA amount–$1 million) December 2018 (increase in TA amount–$0.3 million)
Expected Completion Date	April 2022

---

[18] This figure does not account remaining investment income amounting to $2.3 million, and audit fees and other financial charges amounting to a total of $0.2 million. Accounting for these would result in a net balance of resources amounting to $23.5 million.

[19] Figure reflects cumulative allocations to grant component of investment/technical assistance (stand-alone and linked to loan) projects and direct charges, and includes allocations in 2020 to 6 technical assistance projects and 1 direct charge.

TA 9323-LAO Flood and Drought Mitigation and Management Project

Expected Outcome and/or Purpose	Climate adaptation initiatives integrated in the project design
Expected Results	The TA will support the preparation and project design of the Flood and Drought Mitigation and Management project in Lao People's Democratic Republic, in particular, incorporating climate adaptation initiatives to reduce the impacts of extreme weather events caused by climate change. The project aims to improve climate resilience and livelihoods of agricultural communities through harnessing flood water and reducing damages, improving water reliability during droughts, modernizing agrometeorological information systems, and improving nutrition awareness and facilities.

TA 6627-REG: Building Institutional Capacity: Delivering Climate Solutions under Operational Priority 3 of Strategy 2030

Committed Amount	Climate Change Fund - $2,000,000
Commitment Date	December 2020
Expected Completion Date	November 2023
Expected Outcome and/or Purpose	Implementation of climate actions in Asia and the Pacific increased
Expected Results	The TA will deliver the following outputs: (i) support to developing member countries in incorporating climate change and resilience in long-term strategic planning and projects provided; and (ii) knowledge on climate change-related concepts and tools improved.

2020 Committed Projects and Direct Charges

Projects

ADB Approved Number	Project Name
TA 6683-REG	Support to Climate-Resilient Investment Pathways (SCRIPts) in the Pacific
TA 6598-BHU	Preparing Renewable Energy for Climate Resilience
TA 9323-LAO	Flood and Drought Mitigation and Management Project
TA 6627-REG	Building Institutional Capacity: Delivering Climate Solutions under Operational Priority 3 of Strategy 2030
TA 6663-PAK	Strengthening Food Security Post-COVID-19 Pandemic and Locust Attacks
TA 6661-PRC	Customized Low-Carbon Development Models in Rural and Small and Medium-Sized Towns

Direct Charges

Project Name
PRC: Developing National Strategy for Climate Change Adaptation 2035

BHU = Bhutan, COVID-19 = coronavirus disease, LAO = Lao People's Democratic Republic, PAK = Pakistan, PRC = People's Republic of China, REG = regional, SDCD = Climate Change and Disaster Risk Management Division of the Sustainable Development and Climate Change Department, SDSC = Office of the Cluster Head of the Sustainable Development and Climate Change Department.

46 FINANCIAL SECTOR DEVELOPMENT PARTNERSHIP SPECIAL FUND (FSDPSF)

Donor: Luxembourg, Asian Development Bank

Year Established	2013
Financing Products	Grant, Technical Assistance (TA)
Objective	Support financial sector operational areas of focus, including (i) financial sector development, (ii) inclusive finance, and (iii) infrastructure finance.
Eligible Sectors	Finance
Fund Manager **Alternate Fund Manager**	Junkyu Lee, Chief of Finance Sector Group, SDSC-FIN Arup Chatterjee, Principal Financial Sector Specialist, SDSC-FIN

Financial Position as of 31 December 2020
(Amount in $ million)

Cumulative Donor Commitment	Net Balance Available for Trust Fund Committee Allocation		Number of Projects Funded (Approvals)	Number of Projects Funded (Commitments)
Amount	Amount	% of Commitment		
23.01	2.13	9%	49	48

Featured Project

TA 9496-KAZ: Support to Small and Medium Enterprises and Entrepreneurship Development	
Committed Amount	$225,000
Commitment Date	5 February 2018
Completion Date	28 February 2020
Results	(i) Dedicated small and medium-sized enterprises (SMEs) database created for the Akimat of Kostanay region and successfully integrated into existing digital systems employed by the Akimat. The database serves as a management information tool for designing, implementing, and reviewing the SMEs and Digital Kazakhstan support policies and programs. (ii) Roadmap and action plan to promote SMEs and entrepreneurship development in the region produced and submitted to the Akimat of Kostanay region. Town hall meetings and SMEs survey conducted served as inputs for the roadmap. (iii) Training and capacity building programs for local entrepreneurs, government officials, and staff of financial institutions delivered. These programs focused on financial literacy, marketing and sales, and digitalization of public services.

2020 Committed Projects

ADB Approved Number	Project Name
6532	REG: Promoting Digital Finance Solutions for Inclusive Finance among Partner Financial Institutions
6552	BAN: Strengthening Bangladesh Infrastructure Finance Fund Limited
6554	KAZ: Kazakhstan Green Investment Finance Project
6581	BHU: Strengthening the Financial Market Development Program
6677	BHU: Rural Finance Sector Development Program
6687	PRC: Supporting Sustainable Finance and Regional Cooperation
9333	INO: Promoting Innovative Financial Inclusion (PIFI) (supplementary)
9364	REG: Strengthening Financial Sector Operations in Asia and the Pacific (supplementary)
9627	KGZ: Preparing the Promoting Economic Diversification Program (supplementary)

BAN = Bangladesh, BHU = Bhutan, INO = Indonesia, KAZ = Kazakhstan, KGZ = Kyrgyz Republic, PRC = People's Republic of China, REG = regional, SDSC-FIN = Finance Sector Group of the Sustainable Development and Climate Change Department.

GLOSSARY

ADB committed amount

Amount of projects approved and signed by ADB

contribution commitment

Contributions committed by financing partners in United States $ equivalent valued at exchange rate as of signed cofinancing agreement date

cumulative disbursements

Total amount of project expenditures and administrative expenses paid out from the fund

global funds

Funds for which an organization acts as their global trustee or administrator. They typically leverage a variety of public and private resources in support of international initiatives, enabling the development partner community to provide a direct and coordinated response to global priorities.

net available balance for allocation

Amount available for fund committee's allocation to new projects and/or activities

project and TA commitment

The financing approved by ADB's Board of Directors or management for which the legal agreement has been signed by the borrower, recipient, or the investee company and ADB

special funds

Funds as defined in Article 19 of Agreement Establishing the Asian Development Bank

trust funds

Means of channeling cofinancing resources to finance various projects and activities that meet certain eligibility criteria